HUMAN NATURE
AND CHRISTIAN MARRIAGE

Human Nature
and Christian Marriage

WILLIAM P. WYLIE

ASSOCIATION PRESS

New York

That dear old dreamy bachelor notion—that notion that the unity of marriage, the being one flesh, has something to do with being perfectly happy, or perfectly good, or even with being perfectly and continuously affectionate! I tell you, an ordinary honest man is a part of his wife even when he wishes he wasn't. I tell you an ordinary good woman is part of her husband even when she wishes him at the bottom of the sea. I tell you that, whether two people are for the moment friendly or angry, happy or unhappy, the Thing marches on, the great four footed Thing, the quadruped of the home.

G. K. CHESTERTON

CONTENTS

ACKNOWLEDGMENTS

The passage on the opposite page is from Maisie Ward, *Return to Chesterton*, and is quoted by permission of Messrs Sheed and Ward and Miss D. E. Collins.

The four lines from Charles Williams' *Taliessin through Logres* on page 56 are quoted by permission of the Oxford University Press.

ONE

Human Nature

WHY do men (and women too) have such an incurable tendency to make rude jokes? It seems to be a quite inescapable part of human nature to be ribald about the 'unmentionable'. Partly of course it is the emergence of that adolescent who lies buried in the heart of every one of us; the childish glee which loves to come out bluntly and crudely with that which is normally kept hidden; the desire to shock the complacency and hypocrisy of our elders. Partly it is the joy of the small boy who lets out—always at the wrong moment—the amusing truth that lies below our pomposities.

Viewed like this the tendency to rude jokes becomes a part of that whole world of humour which relies for its effect upon the likening of human beings to animals or vice versa. The talking pig, or the man who looks like a hippopotamus, are only more respectable variants in the same genre. After all in sexual activity men and women are behaving, on one plane at least, precisely like animals. But this offends our dignity. Therefore it is assumed to have a funny side, just as a man losing his dignity by slipping on a banana-skin will always provoke roars of laughter from the onlookers.

C. S. Lewis, in his book *Miracles*, points however to a deeper side to these truths. He suggests that all men and women have a knowledge, instinctive but unconscious, that, for us humans, sex is not just natural. For if it were plainly natural and 'ordinary' then we should neither be secretive nor snigger. But it is just because we feel in our bones that

sex is not just natural that we take refuge from the embarrassment of this obscure knowledge by labelling it as funny, or
disgusting, or both at once. But it is just this obscure knowledge which raises us above the merely animal level; for it is
knowledge that sex, like every other possibility or function
of humanity, is really spiritual or sacred. Dimly we *feel* this;
but until this knowledge is brought out into the open and
acknowledged we shall continue to regard sex as a subject
for rude and secret humour—secret humour because it covers
the embarrassment of dealing with something we don't really
understand.

To start a bawdy rhyme with the phrase, 'It's only human
nature after all', is like whistling or shouting to keep one's
courage up; it is the confession of a basic uncertainty. Uncertainty as to whether in fact it is *only* human nature after
all; for we have a hidden fear that there may be a great deal
more in sex than we realize . . . more even perhaps than we
desire. It seems that almost in spite of themselves men and
women are forced to ask the fundamental question: is there
more in human sex than just this animal imitation? It is
true that only religion, in the end only the Christian religion,
can give a satisfactory answer. But it is human nature itself,
in one of its most characteristic and universal traits, which
poses the question.

The proper place then for us to start our enquiry into the
Christian view of sex and marriage is with the Christian
view of human nature. 'What is man?' Better still, in the
words of the Psalmist, 'What is man that thou art mindful of
him?' Most of us take the word 'mindful' as meaning
that God 'remembers' man, and individual men and
women. But surely it means much more than that. It must
mean that God's mind is 'full' of purpose for man. What
then, in the light of his creation by God, and of God's
eternal purposes, is man?

But once we start thinking about man from this angle we shall find ourselves on a completely opposite track from that of the contemporary world. Both in practice and in theory the modern world sets out to answer this question as to the nature of man (as all other questions too) with no reference at all to God. In practice we live in an age wherein men and women are more and more being thought of as mere units in some system which is considered to have an absolute value in itself. Thus there is 'economic man'; that is, men and women considered simply and solely as units of production or consumption. The ultimate forces being finance and profit, men and women are mere 'hands' or 'consumers'. Again two wars have forced upon all the concept so well described in the first War, that men existed primarily to be 'cannon-fodder'. We may have overcome the Fascist or Nazi idea of men and women as mere units in the all-important Group or Race, but the whole ideology of Communism is that of the unimportance (indeed the essential unreality) of the individual as compared with that of the State or the Hive. Persons are now supposed to be mere ephemeral units in an impersonal greater whole. 'These things cannot happen here', so we say in our insular complacence. But, even while we say this, we regiment ourselves more and more by the twin powers of bureaucracy and advertisement-propaganda. There are many thinkers who hold that the sexual licence of modern times, which the moralists are always deploring, is not at all due to any increase in wickedness. Rather is it due to a very proper and human revolt against regimentation and frustration. Sex is a part of human nature; but it is rapidly becoming almost the only part left in which we are free to be really and fully human. A nation of 'button-pushers' and 'pen-pushers', a people who are so chivvied around that they cannot any longer be human in their ordinary daily life, have now got no place left in which they can express their essential humanity except their amours. But all this, while it amply proves what we knew already, that sex is part of essential human nature, also proves that it is only a *part*. The sexual troubles of this generation spring fundamentally not from being too human, *but from not being human enough*.

So much for practice. But theory also tends to go astray because of the ever-increasing specialization of scientific knowledge. It is now possible to make very detailed and exhaustive study of men and women from a great many different angles; economic, biological, medical and psychological. All this adds enormously to our knowledge; but, while this must be of great value, it also tends to do two other things. It concentrates on one part or aspect of human nature to the exclusion of the whole; and it divides the functions of what should be regarded as a whole. No one will, we hope, attempt to deny that all these studies are of enormous value to our understanding both of humanity and of ourselves. But man is *more* than just a delicate piece of anatomy, he is more than a 'conscious plus a sub-conscious plus a bundle of instincts and complexes', just as he is more than just an economic or a social or a political unit. He *is* all these things of course, and he behaves in part at least in accordance with the ways such things behave, but fundamentally he is much more; *for man is a person*. According to the Christian tradition, which more and more people to-day are coming to recognize is the only full and freedom-giving explanation of human nature, man is a person; a person who possesses both will and freedom. We cannot now go into the age-old controversy of free will versus determinism, save to say that Christianity maintains firmly that, within however limited a field, we all possess both free will and responsibility. It is the possession and the exercise of these twin powers that in fact makes us human. And it is the person who exercises these, the whole person, who is of supreme and absolute value. Of supreme value to God; and therefore of supreme value to all other persons. We cannot stay to argue these points, they must just be taken for granted as part of the Christian tradition. But they happen to be of a quite fundamental importance to any examination of the nature of human sexuality, or of love between men and women, or of marriage which arises out of these two. For marriage is the free union of two fully free and fully functioning persons. It is from the meaning of personality and freedom that there spring at once both the glories, and the tensions, of marriage.

Most of our modern troubles spring ultimately from this separating of men and women into separate parts, and then trying to treat them either as if one of the parts were the whole person, or as if the whole person were merely a casual collection of unconnected pieces. It happens over many things, but sex can shed a very illuminating light upon the whole process. R. H. Ward in *A Gallery of Mirrors*[1] has some very apt comments on this false attempt to isolate men and women into separate parts. First of all he says:

'Love is the concern of the whole man, and neither intellect, nor emotion, nor the senses is the whole man. It is a criticism of the contemporary western person that he is prone to live, not in the whole of himself, but now in his mind, now in his feelings, and now in his body, so that his selves are thus separated one from another and lead their own independent lives, making their characteristic relationships, "falling in love" on their own accounts. Many disastrous marriages may result from believing that one's sexual self is oneself, and its infatuations love'.[2]

One might wish perhaps that the last sentence had been phrased differently, for it is our contention that one's

[1] Gollancz, 1956.   [2] p. 137.

'sexual self' is, or ought to be, one's whole self functioning sexually, but the general picture is extraordinarily true. Ward follows this up with an apt anecdote of personal experience. Obliged to help a drunken semi-prostitute from a public house to her flat, he says that his sexual self drove his other selves away, and so he went up to her room. There, his emotional self taking charge, his feelings quickly changed to pity and he hurriedly left her. On the way downstairs the intellectual self took charge and wanted to know what all the fuss had been about. But had not the other two parts of his 'self' been sufficiently strong, then the first part might easily have lead to an action which the full self would later on have violently repudiated. Such is the danger of trying to live in watertight compartments.

Man is a person of infinite value to God; hence the redemption. He ought therefore to be treated as of infinite value by all other persons. And man was made for happiness. This statement is not quite as simple as it sounds, but it is as well to state quite firmly that Christianity, in its original and proper form, has always insisted that man was made both to desire happiness and to pursue it. It is quite true that there is another side to Christianity. It is pretty true also that the theologians have very effectively hidden the idea of happiness by calling it beatitude. But that only means that final and lasting happiness is never to be found here, but is reserved for eternity and heaven, which fact is of course going to alter the whole balance of the pursuit of happiness by any individual man or woman. We are so made that we want to be happy, and will always seek to be so; that is the prime fact of human nature as, so Christians believe, it was created by God. This is important, for it means not only that there is nothing wrong in wanting to be happy and in trying to be; it also means that there is in itself nothing wrong in anything that can make for human happiness. I want to be happy; you want to be happy; and we can none of us be really happy alone, either.

Now it is true that sex seems to most of us to offer greater opportunities for happiness than almost anything else. But while that means that sex is good in itself, it must also mean that in order to find real happiness, sex must be understood; *and sex in human being is fundamentally different from sex in animals.* This is a second great factor in human nature. Because a man is a person possessing freedom, will and responsibility his sexual functioning must be different from that of the animals. As Mgr Fulton Sheen says in his book *Peace of Soul:*[1]

'The equation of man with the animal is a great fallacy. Sex in man is not the same as sex in animals . . . In the animal sex is mechanical, a matter of stimulus and response. In man it is linked with mystery and freedom. In the animal it is only a release of tension; in man its occurrence is determined by no natural rhythm, but by the will. . . .'[2]

'(In man) . . . desire is from the beginning informed with spirit, and never is one experienced apart from the other . . . Sex instinct in a pig and love in a person are not the same, precisely because love is found in the will, not in the glands.'[3]

Bishop Sheen has a casual reference here to one of the most important differences between mankind and the animals, yet one which is curiously overlooked; the fact that in most mammals sex is seasonal. In man it is not so; that is, sex in man is not seasonal, temporary, a thing limited by outside circumstances. This involves men and women being *troubled* about sex for the whole of their virile life, of course. But the very possibility of feeling troubled is itself a raising above the

[3] Blandford Press, 1950.   [2] p. 155.   [3] p. 165.

merely biological level; the sense of trouble or guilt—whether moral or psychological—being something that only a being endowed with freedom and responsibility could possibly possess.

It has also been suggested that the almost universal, and extremely ancient, human prohibition against incest is the first and most fundamental step away from sex regarded as a merely biological activity. Incest does not bother the animals; it *always has* bothered human beings,[1] for the simple reason that humans have already raised sex into an intimate connection with personality which altogether transcends its merely reproductive function.

But we could go much further than this. Jean Guitton in his book *Essay on Human Love* asks us to consider what happens to the universal instinct for reproduction of the species—what we commonly call the 'sex urge'—when it encounters, or is filtered through, a human consciousness instead of a mere animal instinct. It becomes, he says, something quite different. Considering the way in which the licentious male at any rate is always seeking for self-justification on the lines that sexual desire is a mere biological urge similar to that which occurs naturally in the animal kingdom ('It's only human nature after all') then if there be a fundamental difference it is as well that we should recognize it.

Let us take the picture of a ray of light falling on a prism, passing through it, and then being broken up into separate strands of different colours moving in a different direction. Imagine that the ray of light represents the primal urge of all living things; the instinct to reproduce the species. The prism then represents the specifically human consciousness. What happens to the instinct now? Just like the ray of light it is split into different streams, and a little examination of the actual way in which men and women behave—and always

[1] Cf. Leslie Paul, *Nature into History*, Faber & Faber, 1957: Chapter 5.

have behaved—will show that there are three such streams, three things, that is, which the sex instinct in humans can do, or rather three things which men and women can do with their individual sex instinct.

The first of these, and in some way the most astonishing, is the non-functioning of sex as such. Animals, being mature, immediately mate according to season and opportunity. If they are sterile it is because they have been castrated by men; that is they have had continence forced upon them from above. But human beings both can and do refrain from sexual activity from some force within their own being. This works of course in one of two ways. There is *conscious* control, which is exercised by the will, whereby a man or woman refrains from sexual activity either permanently or for long periods of time. (As a matter of fact few, if indeed any, humans indulge in sexual activity every time they feel the desire. Even the most licentious of men have periodic control.)

Then there is what we call repression, that unconscious inhibition which prevents a person from sexual activity. This latter is not a matter of the will at all, and therefore has no moral significance, but it is a restraint imposed from within, not from outside.

Both these are things of which animals are completely incapable. No animal is a consecrated virgin or celibate; no animal practises even limited self-control, why should it? Nor does it appear (in spite of the American professor who traced canine stomach ulcers to 'faulty relationships with other dogs'[1]) that animals suffer from sex repressions either.

But even when the sex instinct does function, it always with human beings follows one of two streams which are quite different in kind from animal functioning. There is first of all the deliberate indulgence of the sex instinct completely divorced from any biological purpose whatever—sexual

[1] See report in *The Daily Express* for February 22, 1957.

activity pursued simply as an end in itself, purely for the pleasure of the individuals concerned. Contraceptive measures of some kind will be used here, and in some form or other they are as old as the hills. It would be foolish to suggest that animals do not come together sexually for pleasure. Of course they do; but a definite biological purpose is always involved, and usually follows automatically. It is only human beings who can of set purpose cut this out and ignore it while at the same time *consciously* pursuing sex for its own ends.

(It is perhaps worth noting here that some zoologists suggest that, among animals, it is only among human beings that the female is able to obtain equal pleasure to that of the male. Even on what some would, quite wrongly, call the lowest plane, it would seem that *combined* pleasure is a purely human perquisite.)

This pursuit of sex for pleasure only has been a characteristic feature of human life from the earliest times; as witness the euphemism for the prostitutes' business: 'the oldest profession in the world'. There is something here of great importance. We often apply animal terms, half humorously, to men or women of loose life. But this is a completely false use of words. For while, for instance, a female animal is always, by instinct, what amongst humans would be called 'promiscuous', no female animal ever is, or can be, a prostitute.

The third stream from the prism of human consciousness is of course the very opposite of this. *Men and women can transform sex.* What is the difference in behaviour between a tom-cat and a young man, when each of them is driven by the same primal urge of nature; the reproductive instinct? The cat goes 'out on the tiles' and squeals. The young man may of course go and do something very similar. But he is equally capable of behaviour of a very different kind. He may go and stand under his girl's bedroom window for an hour or more, mooning round and looking completely stupid. Then he will go home and sit down and try to write poetry. Normally this will be the usual drivel. But the millionth case may produce great poetry that will live for ever. The cat, because it is only a cat, *cannot* do any more than go out and howl. The man, because he is a man, can transform the same urge into something spiritual. Again, the cat will go out the next night and find another female. The man may do that; but he is also capable of turning the same urge into the basis of a happy marriage. For just as no animal can be a prostitute, so no animal can be a great lover. Love, whether it be the tranquility of a happy marriage, or the earthquake of a ' grand adultery ', is possible only for human beings.

Now if we look at the lives and experiences of men and women as we know them, good, bad and indifferent alike, we see that the sexual nature of every man and woman always does work itself out in one or other of these three ways. While many people have functioned in all three ways, every one functions through one or more of these ways. We *must do so*, being human. For, only man, it seems, and that precisely because he is not just a bundle of instincts, only man can stand outside sex and decide what he will do with it. He takes it with him, either up to the heights or down to the depths. But he only does either because sex is an inescapable part of his personality. For him it has ceased to be a mere biological urge; it has become a function of personality.

The attempt to equate human sexuality with animal instinct is thus seen to break down. But that is not to say that there is not a great deal of what we might call parallel activity. Sex may be vastly more than a biological urge, but it still retains its biological purpose—else why do we desire to have babies? It still retains also all the effects which biological maleness and femaleness imply. The raising of sex above the ' merely animal ' is sometimes, by rather pious persons, supposed to imply that men and women are to become so 'spiritual' that they cease to be men and women. This is a very dangerous idea. Not only is it false in fact but, as we shall see later, it is contrary to what seems to have been the express intention of the Creator. All that is meant by maleness and femaleness remains in humanity and, because man is a spiritual person, these things will affect, not merely the bodies, but the whole characters and personalities of both men and women. Men and women are different all through, and what a lot of trouble would be avoided if a few simple factors implied in maleness and femaleness were remembered! Wives need to remember that it is the nature of the biological male to be the hunter, and that therefore all men, no matter how chaste or faithful, have the deep hunting instinct for variety and for the chase. And how many men fall into trouble by forgetting that it is the part of the female to want to be possessed, to belong to someone, to cling? Many marriages go through quite unnecessary strain because wives expect their husbands to think and behave as women think and behave, and vice versa.

Men and women are persons, free and independent; responsible beings·of infinite value. And at the very basis of their personality there lies the sexual division. To say that our Christianity must somehow integrate sex is to state no more than the obvious; sex is already there whether religion likes it or not. But the way in which sex contributes to the personality, and still more to the functioning of personal relationships, is perhaps a little surprising at first view. The primary potentiality of all personality is communication. (God, we believe, is 'personal', simply because we also believe that He is self-giving to other persons). To be able to enter into communication with other persons *is* personality. But there are two things to be remembered here. First, that no one develops their full personality alone. Contact with others is necessary; and

secondly, it is on the quality of the surrounding group, and
the effectiveness or otherwise of the communication, that the
full integration and quality of the growing personality will
depend. That is why we find that it is a broken home, or the
home of bad quality, that often lies behind the delinquent child
or the adult criminal. Personality is a possibility for every
child as soon as it is born; but personality only comes to
maturity through relationship. Now the moment we mention
the word 'relationship' we bring in sex. For sex is primarily
a relationship, as we affirm every time we use that rather unpleasant euphemism for *coitus*, to 'have relations with'. But
sex can also attempt to *deny* relationship; for it is one of the
many ways in which men and women can do to each other
that which is the most inhuman and cruel of all things—treat
another person in an *impersonal way*; regard them as an object,
a thing, and not a person. It happens of course in many ways,
but we seem to be peculiarly prone to it over sex, and it can
perhaps most easily be seen and appreciated in the sexual field.
It is this which is the real root evil in the whole business of
prostitution. It is not the indulgence, nor the lack of control,
nor the possibilities of disease or of unwanted children, which
are the real sin. No, it is the terrible impersonality of a trans-
action by which each treats the other as a mere object; an
object of desire or relief on the one hand, an object of gain
on the other. It is an attitude which kills the true personality
of each.

But it is when we ask how all this growth of communication
and personality develop that we shall find that sex is mixed up
in it in such an extraordinary way. For it comes in almost
before we are aware of it . . . and that quite apart from the
merely physical effect of hormones etc. We owe the insight into
this to Dr Gilbert Russell and his book *Men and Women*. He
points out that to the very small child communication of personality can only be known through *physical* contact, 'When

we say to a child "Love pussy", what we mean is "Stroke her".' Up to the age of about ten years 'love', which is the highest form of communication, is known *only* by physical contact. And, in spite of their obsessions, we must agree with the Freudians that physical contact is ultimately always sexual. But Dr Russell then points to the next ten years, the decade roughly between ten and twenty. It is during this stage he says that we first begin to appreciate communion and communication apart from the purely physical. Spiritual encounters of all kinds, and a purely mental or spiritual affection and friendship, now become possibilities. We are, as we develop, learning both the possibility and the worth of the non-physical. Dr Russell does not specifically mention it, but the interesting thing is that this is happening at the very time when physical sexuality is developing, and physical sex desire is appearing. Is this the reason why, in the adolescent, sexual desire is so often felt *apart from any personal emotion*? Moralists of the old school were apt to condemn this perfectly natural phenomenon as a mere arising of animal desires, something to be sternly repressed. But may it not be that the real reason for this ' impersonality' of the strong sex desires of the human male is entirely due to the fact that he feels sex as a thing in itself just because the possibility of a higher relationship is also beginning to dawn upon him? Many a youth, fallen into the storm of ' calf-love ', say that he cannot even think of ' that sort of thing ' in connection with the vision of beauty that has burst upon him. (Of course this may be partly due to an unwise upbringing over sex; he may think of sex as essentially nasty and horrid, and that she must not be debased by such ' impure thoughts '.) But the real reason for this strange separation which the adult and mature man will laugh at so cruelly, is that the young man is now learning the full possibilities of communication in two forms, and on two levels. *And they must be learnt separately*, or neither will ever be learnt properly.

That is why premature sexual experience may kill or damage the full possibility of ever learning spiritual communication. That is why more and more marriage counsellors are finding that the cause of so many marriage breakdowns lies in teen-age promiscuity.

But, when both these experiences of communication have been learnt apart from each other, then, somewhere about the beginning of the third decade of life—or earlier in very many cases—they fuse together in the first 'real love' or at any rate in the first romantic kiss. For this first real kiss is the normal way of realization of the final truth; that the most spiritual of relationships expresses itself after all through physical means. The young man who staggers home raving 'she let me kiss her' is a nuisance to himself and a bore to his friends. He is overwhelmed by the sudden discovery of something; that a purely physical thrill, which he has probably had many times before, has now acquired a totally new value and meaning. It is not now just the mild titillation of the contact of lips, it is its *meaning*, the meaning of '*she* let me kiss *her*' and therefore we are on those terms which has knocked him off his balance. For while in every field of human activity 'actions speak louder than words', in communication between persons the most powerful means of communion are *meaningful actions*, and, as between unrelated persons of opposite sex, it is always sexual actions that are the most meaningful: or it should be.

TWO

Sex, Love and God

I F the equating of human sexuality with animal instinct is one of the traps of the devil into which sensual men and women wish to fall in order to justify their indulgence, another and equally disastrous idea is the oft-quoted maxim that sex and love are the same thing. Over and over again we hear it said that love, and indeed marriage too, is ' only sex with added trimmings '.

Yet to deny this too hotly may well be dangerous, for there is a very close connection between the two, and it needs sorting out. That love and sex are not the same thing ought to be clear enough when we remember that it is a very common experience for people to have the one without having the other. It is perfectly possible for a man or a woman to have sexual intercourse with each other without the smallest atom of affection or regard being present. It happens practically every time a man goes with a prostitute. That is sex without love.

But it is also possible, and happens very frequently, for two persons to feel passionate love for each other, and yet never to seek to express this love in actions which are even remotely erotic. This may be done in obedience to religious, moral, or merely conventional scruples. Sexual desire and feelings will of course be present; that is only natural. But if these feelings are allowed no outward and active expression, then they are certainly experiencing love without sex.

Love and sex can each be experienced in isolation. Each can

24

be taken as a thing in itself, and can even be thought of as a thing existing in its own right. But at once we have to question that, because it is a universal human experience that neither of them is ever complete without the other; neither exists in its real fulness without the other. Both the examples of conduct given above have one thing in common; they are always frustrating and incomplete. They are fundamentally frustrating because they are known, however unconsciously, to be incomplete. Quite apart from all questions of ethics or morals, it is just the experience of men and women that sexual intercourse indulged in without love or affection is a poor, tawdry and second-best affair. It fails of the full richness possible to sex. It may relieve tensions, it may solve the 'problems of the moment'; but, because of its essential incompleteness, it usually only raises fresh, and even worse, problems for the future. As Bishop Sheen says: human sexuality 'promises something which it cannot completely supply'. This it does because 'the spirit in man anticipates'. Anticipates what? Surely that personal communication, that joining not only of bodies but of personalities, which is what we mean by the word 'love'. Moreover, so strangely are we made that the very pleasures of the nerves which are involved in erotic actions are diminished and lessened if those same actions are not accompanied by an *emotional* pleasure, the kind of emotional pleasure which arises only when two persons make an act of personal self-giving to each other. 'Selfishness', it has been well said, 'cuts even pleasure in half'.[1]

The real truth would seem to be—as indeed we might have expected—that, amongst human beings, sex is only a pointer. It either points on to something else, or it fails to be all that sex can be, ought to be—and is expected to be.

But if sex without love is incomplete, it is perhaps even more

[1] Cf. H. L. Philp: *A Psychologist looks at Sex*. Hutchinson, 1945. Chapters II and III.

true to say that love without sex is missing something which is quite fundamental to its own nature and fulness (love, that is, of course, between unrelated persons of the opposite sex). For if lovers do not, or cannot, express their love and its emotions in the act of physical union, then they know perfectly well that there is something lacking in the fulness of their love. The reasons which prompt this denial may of course be extremely high. It may be *better* for them, and thus more fulfilling in the end, that they do refrain temporarily. That is the whole case for pre-marital chastity. It is also, we may note, the demand of human nature itself, which desires that this fulness shall express itself only in the circumstances which will make for the closest union and achievement of permanence. But any love which is denied *permanently* its sexual expression is, and is felt by the lovers to be, something less than it ought to be and might be. Such a frustration will of course be felt in the temporary denial which should come before marriage; hence one of the tensions of a long engagement.

Sex and love are neither identical nor are they completely separate. What then is the relationship between the two? This can best be answered by asking which of them is the greater; for the greater will be found to include the less.

This should be easy to answer. Love, as it is actually experienced and believed in by all lovers, is an affair of the whole personality. Anything less than this is only a love of a part by a part. But sex, while it springs from the deep roots of personality, while it affects the whole personality, is, in its properly restricted sense, an affair only of the senses, (using that term to include both the bodily sensations and the emotional excitements). Obviously then that which is an affair of the whole personality must be greater than that which at least functions through only a part. But there is more than that to be considered. Sex, in its ordinary sense at least, will wither and die. Inevitably, as life goes on, it will assume a less and less important place. But love need not die, nor even wither. That it will change we shall have plenty of reasons for showing, but the changes will be only those of a growth into a new kind of dimension a maturing into a different, but related, kind of experience. Love indeed can always go on growing. Its temperature may, as we say, cool down; but the area affected by its heat can be for ever widening. Indeed it is really only that love which has been rooted and grounded in the fullest sexual experience which grows best when sex itself begins to fade. The old mediævals who said that love was the lily that sprang from the dung-hill of sex were very nearly right. They need not perhaps have used such a crude term, or one with such unpleasant associations. But the lily *does* grow out of the dunghill, it feeds on it, it has its roots deep buried in it. Even so, the love which is rooted and grounded in the closest union of sex is the love which flowers best and lasts longest. At the end it may seem to be, indeed it will be, almost independent of sex. But it has only done what the lily has done; it has *grown out of sex, not grown away from it*. Love, then, is the bigger, the more impor-tant, the enduring thing. If sex be a pointer, then it is to love that it points as to the completion and fulfilment of itself. What sex promises is union; union of spirit symbolized by, and indeed made by, union of body. It is the union which alone counts, but without full union on the bodily plane, full union of personalities is for ever impossible.

But true as this may be, there are still many traps for the unwary. Men and women may seek union of personality, but union of a restricted kind. They may be unwilling, or unable, to give full commitment to each other. And then, because of the calls of their bodily nature, may try to express this ' union of a limited kind ' in sexual actions. But this is confusing the whole and the part; it is using for a partial union that which ought to be the means of a complete union.

And as such it must be always unsatisfactory, and is the most frequent cause of heartbreak and tragedy.

Or again men and women may be seeking a real union, dimly comprehended and desired, but may seek it *primarily* through that sexual union which is the more easily achieved. But that is putting the cart before the horse: it is hoping to make a fuller union out of something which is done at one level only. It is probably this which so many men and women are after in their illicit amours and love-affairs; and we need to remember that, if it is full personal union for which they are seeking, then, however wrong the approach, they are nevertheless on the right track. They are genuinely looking for something which will enrich and complete their lonely and frustrated personality. But in approaching and seeking it *primarily and exclusively* through sex, they are almost literally starting off on the wrong foot. For they are hoping that the greater will come from the less. It never does.

For the real place of sex is as an ingredient of a much fuller and deeper union than either of these, a union desired at every level, wherein every part of the personality is prepared for commitment. When a union that is desired in this way is expressed at the sexual level, then it begins to turn itself into a reality. The reality can only come perhaps through sexual union; but it is both envisaged and desired at a level beyond the sexual *before* the sexual action is taken.

The real truth is 'that sex at its highest and at its best can be the means, the sign and the symbol of that enduring love in and through which two persons can come to a fulfilment that neither of them could ever achieve alone'.

There are two important things to note about this quotation. First the word 'can'; it is not automatic; it is always only a possibility. But, until and unless we reject it, it always remains a possibility. Note also the words 'neither of them could ever achieve alone'. For this does not beg the question of those called to live a single life; or of those compelled to do so, and who have accepted their lot. It says only that *for these two*, that is for persons definitely called to what we might term the 'double-harness-life', no complete fulfilment is possible except through that union which is in fact rooted and grounded in sex.

Sex is thus, as we might say, assumed into, or merged into, love. While it lives, and as long as it lives or is active, it does not cease to be itself, nor to have its own characteristic— some would say 'animal'—desires and tensions, but its real purpose and meaning can now be clearly seen. Sex only exists to be an ingredient of something deeper and more lasting. *For while sex indeed may die, that which is made out of sex lives on.*

Now if this is what sex can be, then surely this is what it ought to be. Even if such a fulfilment occurs only rarely, it must always remain as the possibility that lies wide open to the sexual nature of every person. As a matter of fact, of course, it occurs quite frequently, and approximations to it are to be seen all around us. If sex really can mean all this, if this is what it seems to be for in human nature, then we can surely take the further step and say that *this is what God made sex for.*

We might pause here to take a look at the very common misunderstanding of the Christian view of sex, or of the way in which the Church is supposed to look at sexual activity and sexual desire. It is still widely believed that Christians are afraid of sex, or that our religion teaches that everything connected with sex is somehow evil. We have not yet suc- ceeded in dissipating the cloud of misunderstanding that, from the earliest times, seems to have hung over this whole matter in the minds of very many excellent, holy and other- wise intelligent people. One can still find it suggested for instance that the 'sin of Adam and Eve' was something

connected with sex. We can say outright that all competent
theologians of all Christian Churches would to-day hotly deny
any such idea. That God created all things good is after all
the fundamental Christian belief about the nature of the world
and of matter. Sex is, on the natural plane, the means of
reproduction, and, since God created the human race and
presumably wishes it to go on, sexual intercourse must sometimes at any rate be the fulfilling of the intention and will of
God Himself.

Why has the Church, then, been afraid of sex, for no
one can deny that it has been? The thing which the Church
really fears of course is *not sex but sin*, and we have by now
some understanding of what sexual sin really is. If this real
union of personalities is the primary purpose of sex, what
in fact God created it for, then any lesser use of sex, any
practices or attempted experiences which would minimize, or
militate against, such a complete fulfilment, must quite plainly
be wrong. They would in fact fulfil the classic definition of sin,
which is the use of anything at all against or contrary to what
is its God-intended purpose.

It is on this fact, of course, that the case for chastity really
rests. It is not just that unchastity is self-indulgent, or that
it may do much harm, psychological and emotional if not
physical, to one or both of the parties concerned. The
Christian condemnation of unchastity rests on the belief that
it will most certainly risk and endanger that proper consummation for which sex was created. It risks the possibility that
we may later on find ourselves unable to achieve that perfect
personal union for the sake of which God gave us our sexual
nature. Over and over again we are being told that the most
frequent cause of marital disharmony is the unchastity before
marriage of one or both of the partners. Here surely is our
answer to the person who is unable to marry for some years
and who is tempted to unchastity by the specious argument

that 'half a loaf is better than no bread'. It may be so in many walks of life; but here we can say quite definitely 'half a loaf may well turn out to be poison'.

We have now, it will be seen, really brought God into our argument. Up to now we have been looking at everything through human eyes, seeing how human nature really works. But now we are starting to think of how God originally intended it to work; of His divine purposes in creating men and women in the strange way in which He has. It is after all Christian marriage that we are after, and so, from now on, we must think a great deal about God and His will, while keeping our feet, we hope, firmly on the ground of ordinary human experience.

It is one of the greatest tragedies of the present time that the Christian Church seems to have so completely neglected the idea of what we call 'romantic love'. The natural, but highly unfortunate, result has been that the modern world has retaliated by seeming to think of nothing else—as a visit to the nearest cinema will quickly show. And our modern world, having of course almost completely neglected or forgotten God, can only start its thinking about love from the point of view of merely human experience.

That might be all very well if we took only the best of human experience, or if we thought of the whole life-long history of love from the first kiss to golden wedding. But we don't; we confine ourselves instead to that which is only the birth or the beginning. We take the glamour-experience of 'falling in love' and then concentrate upon that as if it were the whole. (Of even this partial experience our films and novels seem to take note only of the most glamorous and emotional aspect). The men of the Middle Ages were in one sense wiser than we are; they always began their thinking about anything from the fact of God. From what they knew— or thought they knew—about God and His nature, they tried to deduce how the same things would work out in this world of men and women. Can we do this over love? It will mean of course that we must start by considering, not love as we know it—or think we know it—but what religion calls the 'love of God'. To quote Bishop Sheen again:

> 'It is the Christian position that the sex instinct is a *reflection* of love in the spiritual order. The sun comes first, then its reflection in the pool . . . All love and all perfection and all happiness are first in God, then in things'.[1]

With the corollary, looking again at the relationship between sex and love, that:

> 'Love includes the flesh; but sex, understood as animal instinct, does not include love. Human love always implies Perfect Love'.[2]

We have already seen the truth of this. We know by now that sex does not include love because *it is sex which exists to be included in love.*

The Christian religion has a great deal to say about what it calls 'love' as applied to God. Not only as love applies to God, but as God, through Christ, gives the same kind of 'love' to His faithful followers. We put the word 'love' in inverted commas because we know, or ought to know, that the English word 'love' is only one translation (and that not under all circumstances the best translation) of an almost new word which the first Christians had to coin in order to describe what they meant. There was something which Jesus said God was, something which Jesus Himself was, something which He gave to His followers and which they had to have between themselves, and for Him, and for God. It was something all-embracing, and the word they coined for it

[1] op. cit., p. 167.   [2] op. cit., p. 168.

in Greek was *agape*. Latin turned this into *caritas*; and another English translation of it is that 'charity' which the
Authorized Version of the Bible uses in the famous passage
of I Cor. 13. More modern translations of the Bible usually
use 'love'. Neither is quite satisfactory because the ordinary
associations of either word—'love' equated with 'glamour'
and 'charity' being an impersonal thing that is 'cold as
charity'—are so unfortunate.   What *agape* really has of course
is both the warmth of love and the width of charity.

Now this 'charity-love' which God has, and which we
ought to have, is a matter of the will: it has little or nothing
at all to do with the emotions or feelings. It means 'wanting
the best' and 'actively doing the best' for others. But if we
examine this love as it exists in God, and as it comes from
God, we shall find as a matter of fact that it has two notes,
and that these two notes can also be found in human
'romantic love', at least as reflections. The first thing implied
in God's love is complete and utter self-giving, self-sacrifice
for the one loved even at the cost of life itself. ('God so loved
the world'; 'greater love hath no man than this'. Christ
died for us, and we must be ready if we are called upon not
only to die for Him but to die for each other.) Love in God,
and love from God, is *always utter self-sacrifice*.

We normally assume that this has no emotional content.
Probably *for us*, painfully and slowly making ourselves love
God, and that neighbour whom we cannot help disliking so
much, it has not. One would hesitate though to suggest that
it had no emotional content when applied to the sacred
humanity of Jesus Christ. If there is any sense at all in the
suggestion that Jesus died on the Cross 'of a broken heart',
one would suggest that the Perfect Man, 'the lord and lover
of men', felt *emotionally* all that we can ever feel of love
for one person . . . *only He felt it for all*. But that means
that there is at least a possibility that 'love' and 'emotional

B

or romantic love' can have a connection. And of course practically every human love-affair shows that there is one: that human love as we said *reflects* divine love. When any young man falls in love there are always two persistent dreams which he has. One is the dream of the bliss that he imagines will come from full contact, physical and also emotional, with his lady; what in fact she can give him—or he can get from her—of joy and wonder. But he always has another dream as well; that is the well-known dream of saving her from a runaway horse, or a house on fire, or some other disaster which will involve his risking his own life. A dream in fact of *what he can give to her*. Even if he dies before he can get anything at all from her he will still be satisfied with this— or at least he imagines he would be. It may be true that our sensual nature is such that the first dream often overshadows the second. It is also true that both dreams are, at the moment of which we are thinking, extremely callow, sentimental and out of touch with reality. But they are both real in the sense that they both correspond to a real inherent possibility. They can both be turned into reality in some way; and, again so strangely are we made, unless some definite effort is made to turn *both* into reality, *neither will endure*.

That is one aspect of divine love as it exists in God. The other is perhaps even more important, but it is much more difficult to put into words. Divine love always implies a complete and utter union of personalities. There is only one word that can really be applied to this. Think of the relationship between Christ and the Father . . . 'I and the Father are One'; or of the relationship between Christ and His followers . . . 'Ye in me and I in you'; or of the ideal relationship between Christians and each other . . . 'members one of another' . . . 'one head, one body'. The whole point of Christianity has surely always been that there is a relationship between Christ and the believer in which

neither lives alone, but each lives in and through the other.
The hope of heaven has always been that in the end we shall
be 'partakers of the divine nature', that is, live in and through
God. *Interpenetrating personalities:* that is what divine love
is, that is what it effects and how it works, and that is what
human love at its highest and at its best also wants. It is
strange how even the semi-facetious language of ordinary
life illustrates this. When a man laughingly refers to his wife
as his 'better half' he is unconsciously bearing witness to this
great truth—the truth that those who love are—or at least
ought to be—half of each other.

If then we take this love as it exists in God and look for its
reflection on earth we have little difficulty in finding it. The
only difference is that earthly romantic love between men
and women has in it another element, that of the *first* dream
referred to. It has the element of self-getting, of the physical
and emotional desire to get from the beloved the joy and
wonder and thrill that arises from sex. If that were *all*, then
such love might have to stand condemned or at least separated from love as it is in God. But as we have seen, it need
not be all, in fact it never really is all. Once grant the self-
seeking or emotional and physical part of human love as only
one element, then it can be seen to have a right and proper
place. It is not something *merely* human, merely extraneous;
it is *one* element of a synthesis, and, being a natural part of
human nature, it was itself made and given by God in order
to lead us on to find the other elements.

If we ask why God divided human beings into two kinds,
the male and the female, the normal answer would be that
it was simply in order that the race might go on. If man
is a product of Evolution, as most Christians now fully admit,
then it is obvious that Man shares that sexual division which
runs all through nature. But there is a very strange thing
about sex that was pointed out years ago by that much-

neglected Russian thinker Solovyov. He asks whether we
have ever noticed how, as we go higher in the scale of
Evolution, passion increases and fertility decreases. Fishes
are cold-blooded yet spawn in millions; animals are passionate, but their litter is only half a dozen or so. In human beings
passion is far greater; it is assumed into an emotional and
spiritual relationship. Yet this relationship is every bit as
strong and binding, even if there be no possibility of fertility
at all. Many a couple who are sterile, and know they are so,
have as deep and enduring a love as any other. Why; and
how? Is it possible, he asks, that sex is all the time striving to
get away from mere reproduction? Has it after all a higher
aim?

Some people may be surprised if we now look at a text or
two in the early chapters of Genesis. But surely we can
realize that these old myths may enshrine, in childish language and pictures, some tremendous truths. We are all under
the domination of the Garden of Eden story of Creation; we
forget that there is a rather different account in a later
chapter. We forget also that 'Adam' means 'man', and so
we keep thinking of Adam as an individual . . . either
legendary or partly historical. But if we look at Gen. 5.2, we
shall perhaps get a shock. 'Male and female created he them,
and he called *their name Adam* (i.e. mankind) in the day when
they were created'. *Mankind in its fulness is male and female.*
If we want to be really theological we should look at the
doctrine of the Trinity. Most people would think that this was
the last thing to be thought of in connection with 'romantic
love'. But don't let us be too sure. Purged of all theological
subtleties the doctrine of the Trinity, of God as a Unity in
Trinity of Father, Son and Holy Ghost, means that God, in
His real and inmost being and reality, is 'Persons
in Relation'. 'Interpenetrating personalities' are of the
essence of God. And man, we are told, is made in the image

of God. The most human thing about man is his likeness, not to the animals, but to God. Man then can only really be himself when he too is a relation of interpenetrating personalities. And so man was made male and female, eternally separate from one another, eternally complementary; eternally divided yet eternally attracted; blessing one another and infuriating one another; but ever unable to be their real selves alone. Between them there arises not merely the biological urge for reproduction and the necessary act of coitus, but the strong desire for this act is mixed with the obscure knowledge that only in such a complete union with a person of the opposite sex can any one of us ever be what we might be, or what we ought to be.

What is that? The answer may be found in the words of Jesus: ' They twain shall be one flesh . . . so then they are no more twain '. *Out of two must come one; out of two interpenetrating personalities must emerge a new kind of mystic third person.*

That is what divine love is; that is what the reflection of divine love as seen on earth would be expected to be; and that is what human love sees in its vision and so often makes actual in practice. That, and another thing; the desire and emotion which attract the one to the other *on the plane where human beings first feel things*, the sensitive and emotional one.

Could one put it rather simply and say that, when God ' created ' men and women, He took the already existing biological division of sex (which in nature is imposed on all the higher organisms as a means of producing the variety which Evolution needed to work on) and, with certain important modifications in its nature which we have already noted, adapted and used it as a means of dividing His new ' creation ' into two? Can we say that He divided it so that out of the union of the two separated yet complementary halves there might come something greater, that should be a reflection of His own being and His own infinite love? But it was sex by which He divided it, so that each should yearn for the other and feel incomplete alone, and it is by 'sex-in-love' that humanity can alone be reunited into a greater whole. Sex is the division, but love plus sex are the union; the 'one flesh' of interpenetrating bodies and personalities that reflects God as no other union possibly can.

This may all seem highly theoretical, and even theological. Until one falls in love; and then one sees that it is the plain truth. *For in the end falling in love is just seeing this.*

THREE

Christian Marriage

W E can now begin to understand why it is that the Christian religion so concentrates on marriage rather than on either sex or love. For while Christianity has said remarkably little about love, and scarcely any more about sex regarded as an activity in itself, it has always said a great deal about marriage. The reason is that it is in marriage, and only validly in marriage, that Christianity regards this 'one-flesh-union' as coming into reality. Some people would deny that there is such a thing as 'Christian marriage' on the grounds that, since marriage is meant by God for all men and women, it is therefore a 'natural' thing, not to be confined to Christians at all. Of course it is not; and it might therefore be better to talk about marriage as understood by, practised by, and demanded of, Christians. What we shall be thinking about then, is that kind of marriage—together with the elements and circumstances which will lead up to that kind of marriage—which is laid upon those who desire in some sort at any rate to be faithful to the Christian religion as they understand it.

The trouble and confusion of the present world arises from the fact that, while Christianity concentrates on marriage, our culture concentrates almost entirely upon love. (That is, when it does not concentrate entirely upon that part of love that is composed of sex and glamour.) If we were right in our attempt to analyse love, then we shall see that this absorption of the modern world is an absorption *in the reflection instead*

of in the reality. There is no need at all to deny love in saying
this, only to note that concentration on the reflection, especially in a world where things have the habit of going wrong and
being imperfect, may all too easily lead us astray. For the
moment then we too will concentrate upon marriage itself
and leave love and sex to find their places within this larger
and more fundamental thing.

According to Christianity it is marriage which unites the
separated portions of our broken humanity. It may be said
therefore to do two things, both of which belonged to the
purposes of God in creation. It brings together the two halves
of the complementary being ' man ', ' Adam ', thus making
that new union which alone really shows forth the infinite
glory both of God and of man His image. And it closes that
rift or breach in the human heart which arises from the fact
that every one of us, *qua* mere male or female, is incomplete.
It is meant to do these things; that is what it is for and what
its meaning is. But that does not mean to say that it succeeds
in doing these things in every individual case. Far from it,
indeed, as we know too well; what it does is to offer these
possibilities to every married couple.

We must turn now to the actual words of the Lord Jesus
Himself in instituting (or more properly in re-instituting for
His followers) the state or condition of matrimony. These
words are of tremendous, and in one sense of terrible, import.
' They twain shall be one flesh . . . for this cause shall a man
leave his father and mother and cleave unto his wife . . . so
then they are no more twain but one flesh '. One scarcely needs
to remember the enormous strength of the family and filial
bond among the Jews of His day—and indeed of every day—
to see what Jesus was implying. A man, and presumably this
applies also to a woman, must leave the closest natural bond
of all, that of parents and brothers and sisters, and then be
joined to his wife in a bond that is even closer and more

binding. Now no man can lose his brother or sister except by death; he may hate them like poison and run to the ends of the earth to get away from them, they remain his kin all the same. So apparently does his wife; and even more strongly. There is something in the man-woman relationship in marriage which is a unity stronger than anything else. It is worth noting how the wedding service of the Church of England has got in it a most unfortunate mistranslation, and one which has been productive of an enormous amount of misunderstanding. In that solemn moment when the bride and groom are kneeling before him, the Priest is instructed to join their hands together and say; '*Those whom* God hath joined together let no man put asunder'. The corollary that follows in ordinary thought of course is that if, in a particular case, it seems, to all outward appearance, that God has signally failed to join X and Y together, the rest need not apply. But what Jesus is recorded as saying is rather different. '*What* God hath joined together. . . .' *Not X and Y as individuals*, but the man-woman-one-flesh relationship of *any couple* who happen to enter the state of matrimony.

Of course this raises the whole question of divorce and re-marriage. But here we will concentrate on the positive side of the relationship established by marriage. But how many people have noticed what to the modern mind must seem rather terrible, not to say shocking? *Jesus does not say one word about love.* He never says: 'If they love one another . . . if their marriage is happy . . . if they are successful'. It is all impersonal and applies, so it would seem, to any couple at all quite regardless of their individual feelings or circumstances. And it would seem that the Church, in thus concentrating on marriage and almost ignoring the other factors which we feel to be so important, is yet only following the thought of her Master.

Now if all this corresponds in any sense to reality, we must say that in marriage a *status of relationship* is established. It is a status 'of which God takes cognizance', *about which God does actually do something.* By marriage a relationship is established, not only between the two persons, but between them as a couple and God. And the important word is 'status'. For this is where we all tend to go wrong to-day. Because there is a legal side to marriage, because it has legal forms and promises and responsibilities, we tend to look on marriage as a *contract.* What has happened is really rather interesting. In the old Jewish Church, and in the Christian Church for many centuries, the 'betrothal', which was something considerably more binding than a modern 'engagement', was looked on as a *contract.* It was a contract that the parties would, if other conditions were properly fulfilled, later on enter into the *state* of matrimony. Now, though we still regard an engagement as a contract in the sense that under some circumstances there can be legal redress of 'breach of promise' if the contract is wilfully unfulfilled, we have gone and shifted the idea of contract from engagement and applied it to marriage itself. We have in fact taken 'contract' away from its proper place, and put it in where it does not belong. For marriage is, for Christian thought at any rate, much more than a contract: it is a state of life or a status of being. And this status is *of its own nature,* so we believe, *permanent.* It is permanent because it affects the being and reality of a person as much as, and even more than, being a member of a family determines one's reality and being. Only that which God makes is in the end real; and we say that here is something—the man-woman relationship of marriage-unity—which is made by God and not only by men.

Of course it also has in it the element of contract. It must have, because both the law and society are interested. It is very necessary for us to see how and why these two powers come in. We might say that marriage is so very much a per-

sonal thing that it concerns no-one except the two persons
and God. That in fact is what causes the inevitable tensions
of marriage; both marriage as an institution and marriage as
an experience. The most private and personal thing in the
world has yet to be dragged out into the widest publicity.
More than dragged out. It is most intimate; but it is at the
same time the concern of the community they belong to,
whether State or Church or both.

The reasons are obvious. Whenever two persons enter into
a union in which the possibility of children arises, then all
the questions of law, inheritance, legitimacy, etc. come up
The law and society must have some concern also for the
family-community. Hence the law will only regard as legiti-
mate those children born of a union in which proper
provision is made, and responsibility taken, for them. Two
people want to enter into a close union, but if that union is
going to affect society—as it must if there are children—
society itself must define the kind of union it will recognize.
Hence marriage of some kind, with its inevitable laws and
limitations.

But there is more than that. Human beings are weak and
changeable, at the mercy of crises both exterior and interior.
If a union of two persons is going to have lasting legal and
social consequences, it must be a union both defined in legal
terms *and having legal sanctions for its continuity.* But
these sanctions, which involve in fact a contract of 'permanence' and exclusiveness, fulfil also a vitally important
personal role. *They protect the parties against their own
feelings*; they provide a binding structure within which all that
marriage means can be developed. Some may want to call
them a strait-jacket; but most of us know that nothing can
grow unless it has a structure of some kind.

(The word 'permanence' was put in quotation marks in
the paragraph above for the reason that at the present time

we in this country are in a curiously anomalous position. It is still stated that the law of England means by marriage a 'life-long and exclusive union'. Yet the same law every year returns to about fifty-six thousand persons (the latest figure for divorces is actually twenty-eight thousand per annum) their condition of being eligible for a fresh legal marriage. It is difficult to see how this can be reconciled with the former statement. Dr. Gilbert Russell[1] suggests that, in fact, in law 'the words "for life" mean no more than that no fixed term or provision for termination is *part of the contract*'.

We see here what has in fact happened. Fixing our attention on the perfectly proper contractual side of marriage as if that were all it is, we have dropped the idea of permanence and forgotten that marriage is after all a state of being. To that we must now return, for it is of marriage for Christians that we are thinking.

If marriage is a status, that is, something both made by and intended *by God*, then the entry into that status ought to be in response to the command, will or calling *of God*. And here we must reintroduce that good old word 'vocation'. There was a time when some Christians wanted to limit the idea of a 'vocation' or calling to the ministry of the Church, or the monastic life, or something equally 'pious'. To-day we have perhaps widened the meaning too much when we apply it to any kind of job at all for which a person feels particularly fitted. But, provided we can keep the thought of God in the foreground, the wider we make this word the better. A vocation is that which we are meant to serve God by doing, what we individually are meant to do by Him and for Him. It will probably, almost certainly, be not only something we are fitted to do, but something we are attracted to do and want to do, and, of all vocations, surely this one of being 'one half of a divine unity' is the greatest and most

[1] *Men and Women*, p. 47.

important. We ought however to remember that, if marriage is a vocation, so also for some people single life may be a vocation. Again, in the past some Christians tended to talk as if only single life were a real vocation. We must not run to the other extreme and talk as if only married life were a call from God. God calls every individual in His own way and to his own individual kind of life and service.

Here of course some people will think that we are being altogether too pietistic and unrealistic. 'A direct calling from God'; a religious matter. That is what we say marriage is. *Ask, however, how such a call would be expected to come.* 'By prayer and fasting'? Yes; in one sense that is perfectly true, however widely we interpret the term prayer. But we must never forget that God makes His will known to us in all sorts of different ways. God uses circumstances to guide and direct us; we do not know Him only when we are on our knees. Is it too much to say that the call of God can come when we are on our knees, and also perhaps when we are in someone's arms? May it not truly be said that *falling in love mutually with someone you are free to marry IS God's call to the vocation of marriage?* Of course it must be mutual, that goes without saying. But we added the saving clause 'with someone you are free to marry', because love bloweth where it listeth and we often can, and do, fall genuinely in love with people we are not free to marry. But it is no condemnation or denial of the reality of such love to say that, whatever else it be, it is *not* a call to the vocation of marriage.

Surely this will help us to see what is the proper place of love. For it cannot be too strongly said that *marriage is made by being married, and not by being in love.* This would be true even if marriage were only a legal contract. Two people may be in love, but it is only the legal act of the State and its official which actually makes the contract of legal marriage. It is not love which marries them, it is ' signing on the dotted line '. How much more is this status which we said is made by God Himself? And it is worth noting what are the things which the Christian Church has said actually go to make this status of being married. They are ' consent' and ' consummation'. 'Consent' is the intention, publicly declared and vowed, of living together for life under the exclusive and life-long bonds of marriage. This must be made ' publicly ', that is before representatives of the Church and/or State. ' Consummation' is sexual intercourse between these same two persons. *Both are necessary*. Persons who have sexual relations, but do not make this public consent are not married. Nor are persons who, having made this consent, do not follow it up by the natural and proper union of coitus. That is why, among Roman Catholics, the Pope can dissolve a marriage where there has been no sexual intercourse. Both these things are done by the parties themselves. This is important. You often hear people say, ' Oh, yes, Mr So-and-so married us ' referring to the Christian minister who performed the wedding service. That is not correct. *They married themselves*, for it is they alone who can do these two things which actually make marriage. All that ' Mr So-and-so ' did was to give the blessing of the Church and to pronounce that they were married. This he pronounced on hearing their vows, which imply that there will be consummation. The importance of this lies in the fact that if they had chosen to be married in a Registrar's office instead of in church they would still have entered into Christian marriage. The Church of Rome has its own rules for its own members; but all Churches agree that a marriage in a Registrar's office fulfils the necessary conditions. Those who enter into their union in this fashion are entering into Christian marriage—even though it lacks that public blessing and seal of approval of their Church which all good Christians ought to value. But this merely reinforces what we said above about marriage being made by being married and not by being in love. Love is, in our society at least, *the reason for getting married*. We regard it —not necessarily perhaps absolutely correctly—as the necessary preliminary for marriage; that is, as the normal way in which the call of God to marriage comes. But the marriage is the marriage and *it does not depend upon love for its existence*. There is of course a corollary to all this. If marriage is made by being married and not by being in love, then marriage is not unmade if love ceases. There will be all sorts of problems arising out of this that we shall look at in a later chapter, but we must insist on this now.

We can now begin to see something of the place of love and sex in all this. We have called sex a ' pointer ' and said that it only existed in order that it might point towards, and be included in, love. Now we can see that love also is a pointer; a pointer towards that marriage in which it is its nature to be included, to which it leads and drives us. As was well said once in a lecture to a youth group, ' *Sex and romance and love are meant to be ingredients in the pudding of marriage. They are not snacks to be gobbled on the way* '.

Leaving technical terms aside we might say that the two notes of marriage, and especially of Christian marriage, are *permanence* and *exclusiveness*. Some would of course dismiss those as outworn and arbitrary barriers against full self-expression. Others would say they are so obvious as to need no discussion. But we might profit by enquiring a little further into the reasons for the Christian insistence on these two things. Marriage is the framework, the skeleton, around and within which is to be built the ' one-flesh union ' or *henosis*. This is a word which always comes up when Christian thinkers talk about marriage. The trouble is that, while everyone knows more or less what is meant, no one has as yet been really able to define it.[1] The reason of course is that it is a spiritual reality. One of the best descriptions was that unconsciously given by the lady who was talking about the girl who had recently broken her engagement to someone. She said; ' I am so glad Molly has broken her engagement to John. What a horrid third person they would have made.' She was *not* thinking of any possible child of the marriage; she was thinking of that inevitable unity which arises whenever two people enter into the permanent relationship of marriage.

The late Charles Williams in several of his poems on the theological aspect of romantic love and marriage continually uses the term ' twy-nature '. This again is difficult and defies analysis, but one can see what he means.[2]   The late Canon Hugh Warner used to say that it took about ten years at least to make a marriage. There was first the ' honeymoon period ', and then the ' adjustment period '. During these the children arrived and began to grow up; so that, at some period about ten years after the wedding, there suddenly appeared a new entity which all the world recognized as ' the Joneses round the corner '. (It applies equally of course to childless couples.) In our ordinary common everyday speech we know well that the words ' the Joneses ' and ' the Smiths ', though applied to *couples*, have in each case a *single meaning*. They point to the material, visible and worldly appearance of the spiritual unity. Christianity of course goes on to say that, with Christians, nothing is ever made by them alone. All is made by God working through them; what matters is what God makes out of them . . . if they will let Him. Hence the quite natural Christian suggestion that the essential unity is that which is

[1] There is a very interesting attempt in *The Mystery of Love and Marriage* by Dr Sherwin Bailey, SCM Press, 1952.
[2] For a fuller treatment of Williams' ideas see the author's *Pattern of Love*, Longmans, 1958.

made by God. But it is worth noting that, whether they co-operate with God or not, whether they allow his grace full play or not, *something unique is always made out of every married couple*. It is the happy and successful marriages to which we usually point as examples of this living unity. Thank God these are innumerable; but it is equally true that a unity of some kind is also made by the failures, and seen in the unhappy and broken marriages. Take two people whose marriage has ' reached breaking point '. Friends and observers are apt to say that they have nothing in common, there is no unity at all. They are wrong. There *is* a unity, but it is a unity of mutual failure. Each may be, and so often is, a person of charm and sympathy when with other people. *But put them together* and they at once bring out the worst in each other. There is a mutual discord far greater than anything which either could produce alone. ' One-flesh-gone-sour ' would be a good description of such a couple, but the trouble is that the hell which their home seems to be is a hell which they alone have made, and made out of each other. There is a terrible sense in which they are just as much a unity as are the happiest couple. For just as every individual is unique, so husband and wife become, by virtue of their marriage, a *unique couple*. As such they cannot help but create a ' mystic third person ' who is either better or worse than the two of them alone.

This mystic union (' mystic ' because spiritual and mysterious, yet real enough to be recognized by the neighbours) is made out of the whole of each person. But the whole of me can mean nothing less than the whole of my life; for I am never whole till the day of my death. I bring to my marriage all that I was from birth until then, and then marriage makes the rest of my life, of our joint lives. ' Wholeness ' therefore must mean ' permanence ', and wishing to give the whole (either to another person, or to God, or to both) must mean giving for life. Nothing less than what is left of life is the whole of me, or the whole of the other. But this wholeness, the whole of each for the other, must, for the male-female union, also mean exclusiveness. Each man and each woman is unique; it is as being unique that the individual is himself or herself the 'image of God'. But if we were right in saying that the full image of God is something more than just unique individuals, that the true humanity which reflects the being of God is male-female joined, *then every couple so joined are unique also*. There is no half-way house here. Either this image of God is to be found in the whole human race by any number of men mating with any number of women, or it can be incarnated and found only in absolutely unique and separate couples. Every consideration of biology and sociology, to say nothing of what we know of the nature of love between individuals, points to the latter as being the only valid method. *But this must imply exclusiveness.* Either I reflect this bi-unity of humanity with any number of women—and they with any number of males—or I can make it only with one, and she with me alone. Only then, as we are exclusively and permanently each other's, can we even attempt to make that kind of unity for which God created men and women— for which indeed He gave us both our sexual functions and our romantic emotions.[1]

It is of course this permanence and exclusiveness which give what Dr Gilbert Russell would have called the first 'rules of the game'. He says, in his book *Men and Women*, that marriage is the court in which we are to play the game of being married. But the game has rules. How many marriages have in fact been ruined by not remembering this, or what the rules happen to be? In every walk of life it is true that harmony, satisfaction and fulfilment can come only by fitting

---

[1] This must not be taken as in any way begging the question of the rightness of second marriage after the death of the original partner.

into the frame of rules or circumstances. To fight against them, or to ignore them, always causes frustration and strife.

The first rule of marriage is that marriage itself implies *limitation*. Married people just cannot behave as bachelors and spinsters do, not at least if they hope to remain married. They do not of course want to behave like single persons, at any rate during the honeymoon period. But after that things may change. Indeed they certainly will, and there will come a time when one or the other sighs for the freedoms of single life; when, unless they are careful, one or the other begins to behave with something of the freedom from restriction of single life. We are not thinking of 'illicit affairs' as yet, or anything of that kind, but merely of those freedoms of coming and going and doing exactly what we want that are characteristic of single life. But there is no such freedom now, instead there is limitation and responsibility. The attempt to by-pass these is not only a weakness in itself, it may be the first step towards wrecking the marriage.

But we should note that this limitation, which is an inevitable part of marriage, has also a very important application to life before marriage. Dr Gilbert Russell again in his book *Men and Women* points to both these aspects of limitation when, talking of that 'sexual experience', whose alleged necessity is the bugbear of modern life, he contrasts this so-called 'value of sexual experience' with the other experience of 'coming virgin to marriage'. He goes on to say: 'A man cannot taste *both* the pleasures of promiscuity *and* the knowledge of what it means to be faithful in love'. Both these higher experiences do imply a limitation, which is also the first rule in the game of marriage.

The second rule is that marriage is a work; *a work of art*. If love and sentiment stress the beauty of a work of art, realism must stress the 'work'. Somewhere in his writings that great and religious artist the late Eric Gill says that the mistake we usually make is thinking that the artist is a special kind of man, whereas the truth is that 'every man is a special kind of artist'. We might paraphrase that and apply it to marriage by saying that instead of a successful marriage being a special kind of marriage, every marriage has its own special kind of success. ('Happiness' would be preferred by some, no doubt, but that term might be too question-begging.) Even as it stands it is not, alas, quite true in practice, but it *is* true that every marriage can have, could have, its own special and unique kind of success. But this success is a long drawn out result of hard, mutual, creative effort. The best epigrammatic statement of this truth was the answer given by a discussion group at a youth club in answer to the question, 'What is wrong with the conception of love as usually given in films?' Their answer was straight and to the point: 'Too much hand-holding and too little house-work'. (Not that housework is the chief thing meant by 'creative effort', though it has its place. and even its place as a *mutual* activity.) But the effort needed to make a happy adjustment and joining of two diverse natures is real enough, and on top of it there comes the new joint life that has to be built together. That is. why the simile of a 'scaffolding' or 'skeleton' was so apt for the permanence and regulation side of the institution. That is what marriage is; a scaffolding *within which* some new thing is to be built—built, created evolved, whatever word one chooses it comes to the same thing. But it is a work *of art* in two senses. First that what we desire to make is a beautiful thing; beautiful and unique. Secondly that the actual building requires thought, skill, effort and a cunning hand. 'Not everyone has got them?' No; nor is anyone without some modicum anyway, and we keep on forgetting that there is the grace of God always available. The truth of course is, as Christians ought to know, that the real builder is God. But if God is the builder He still leaves two things to us. *He uses us as His tools, and He thinks the design through our thoughts as far as we will let Him.*

We have stressed already the fact that what makes marriage as a thing in being is, not love, but actually being married. Even more so, what makes a successful marriage is not just love, it is the building of the work of art by the persons in love. They never would have started it, they would never have had any vision of it, if they had not been in love; but what actually builds the work of art is the hard work to which that vision called. This may be the explanation of that strange phenomenon we have all noticed; that some marriages which started off in a blaze of passionate love seem to wither out and die, while others, where the previous love seemed on the surface comparatively mild, have not only endured but have grown in warmth and tenderness. It may be that the first kind rested content in mere love, that they thought, in the common phrase, that all would come right merely by holding hands in the moonlight. The effort did not seem to be needed, and when realization came it was too late. The other started off more realistically with effort. And out of shared effort come first comradeship and then tenderness, *the two things which always outlast passion.*

It is the existence of these rules, and the complete impossibility of playing the game at all except in submission to them, which probably prompted what some people would say was one of the oddest statements ever made by a writer on the subject of Christian marriage. Chancellor T. R. Milford of Lincoln, in his little pamphlet *A Christian Philosophy of Sex,* says this, '. . . it would be better to say to young people —such advice has proved useful on occasions—" It doesn't matter *which* of them you marry—not in comparison with *how* you marry whoever it is "'. This is what the cynical old

Scots doctor in James Bridie's play *It Depends What You Mean* meant when he said that, *if you had to*, you could probably manage with any one of half a dozen girls you found in a cinema queue. Since no one would accuse Chancellor Milford of being a cynic we had better have another look at it before we condemn such a statement out of hand. A real examination shows both sayings to be completely true. For since it is the 'rules of the game' and the working out of these that are all-important, it is very likely that, *if one had to*, one could build something fairly successful with any one of several persons . . . provided of course that the effort was mutual. *Could* do so, because it is the effort and mutual understanding and creative self-sacrifice that matters. None of this is to deny love, for the reply of course is, 'How much more ought one to succeed; how much more beautiful a work of art ought one to be able to create, when one works with one who has also been called by the vision of real romantic love?'

But there is one more rule, or method of playing the game, without which there can be neither success nor happiness (and, whether in marriage or anything else, these two things are not quite the same). The only word for this third thing is 'substitution'. Each has got to live in, and by, and through the other; each has in some sense to substitute his or her own wishes, desires, happiness, and indeed life, by those of the other. This is not easy; but it is really the old, old problem of Christian unselfishness worked out in daily domestic encounter. Christians know that they are commanded to be humble and unselfish. They also know, we hope, that they are *not* commanded to be doormats. For to let other people ride completely roughshod over us ministers to *their* pride, may be the worst thing for them, and therefore is not, by definition, 'willing the best' or Christian 'love'. The 'hen-pecked husband' or the frightened submissive 'little wifie' are not examples of Christian marriage at its best. For the substitution must be *mutual*. Each must learn to submit his or her own will, not merely to the whims of the other, but to the *general will of the two-in-one*. True enough; but it usually has to start by a good deal of real submission to the other . . . and sometimes for a time even to their whims. The 'two-in-one-will', the new 'twy-nature', does in fact only grow as each learns painfully, slowly, hardly, and by no means always joyously, to do what the other wants instead of their own chief desires. There was a phrase we used in the second chapter to describe divine love, of which therefore human love was meant to be a reflection, 'interpenetrating personalities'. There we applied it to love, but this is also precisely what marriage effects or should effect. It is, as we said, the only method of the game of marriage. It is this to which St Paul refers in that strange phrase in Ephesians: 'But I speak of Christ and the Church'. Paul was looking for some recognizable picture of that interpenetration of the Christian by the Lord ('I live, yet not I, but Christ liveth in me'), and the only picture he could find was marriage. So he says they are in a sense both the same thing, and both 'mysteries'.

But if marriage is the only thing on earth like the Christ-Church-Christian mystic union, then it follows that marriage is like nothing else on earth. That will be important enough when we are thinking of the theory of marriage. Here we are concerned with its practical side. Only as each lives in the other, and both live through the growing and developing 'twy-nature', can marriage ever be successful. If we want to quote Scripture again then we may say that it is just as true in love and marriage as in religion that 'he that loseth his life shall find it'—and only he. Charles Williams in his Arthurian poetic saga has three or four lines which perfectly describe the result of this same process:

> '. . . the everlasting house the soul discovers
> is always another's; we must lose our own ends;
> we must always live in the house of our lovers,
> my friend's shelter for me, mine for him.'[1]

Something like this is what lovers imagine in their first rap-
tures; something like this is essential to any success in
marriage. But the poet has given us an insight into something of tremendous importance as soon as we realize that he
has not confined this substitution only to lovers. He does
mention lovers of course; but he includes 'friends'. And for
a Christian this *must in the end include all persons.* Is
Williams suggesting to us that in truth lovers and spouses are
really just special cases of a general rule, as the mathe-
maticians might say? True enough perhaps in theology and
theory, but most of us have to learn the theory by the practice. Are we then perhaps meant to learn the theory by the
practice of the special case; to come at length to the general
through the daily practice of whatever special case is offered
to us? It begins to look rather like it. If we take these three or
four 'rules of the game' of marriage, these things at which
we have been looking, 'limitation of attention', 'creative
effort of will', 'substitution', we shall see that, when properly
practised, they add up to something else. Looked at from
another, and on the surface less romantic and emotional
point of view, they begin to look remarkably like the thing
which Christians have learned to call 'charity'. They have
the marks of divine love as distinguished from mere romantic
love. Yet it is from the latter that they have sprung. Add
now one further dogma and practice, of Christianity; the
doctrine of vicarious sacrifice. The belief that sacrifice by
one person always effects good in, or for, someone else.
There is not a husband and wife in the world who is not

[1] *Taliessin through Logres,* pp. 44-5.

learning by hard daily experience something of what this means.

Can we, then, dare we, say that, for those called to 'double-harness' life, marriage is meant to be the actual way in which they are to learn what divine love and 'charity' mean?

We can now see the most profound reasons for calling marriage a vocation from God. Marriage is meant to be at least one way by which men and women can actually grow in the practice of divine love and sacrifice. It is the means whereby married persons can at least be put on the road to that understanding of God, that union with His essential life and love, to which single persons are to come by a different road.

The cynic laughs at the romantic 'nonsense' of which lovers talk and sing, the 'callow dream' that their emotional love can only end in heaven. But the lovers may be more right in the end than the cynics. All that is needed is for callowness to turn to maturity, for the dream to become the action of marriage. If such lovers follow the authority of their dream then they will continue to try and work it out in practice even when the glamour seems to fade away. But that which they are working out so slowly, so painfully—and often indeed so dully—is, if it leads to charity, the pathway to heaven after all.

Is that what marriage is for? What sex and romance and love were for as pointers? The whole thing seems to hang together as in a pattern. But it is always marriage, which is both the culmination and the practical working out, which is the clue to everything else.

FOUR

The Approach to Marriage

SOMEONE once said that the trouble with so many young people to-day is that they tend to ask questions about sexual matters from the wrong angle. He did not mean that they were leaving out morals, but something rather different. They were asking questions in isolation; talking as if this or that problem were an isolated fact, a thing in itself that could be judged entirely on its own merits.

It is natural perhaps to do so, but it is the completely wrong approach. If all that we have said is anywhere near the truth, then it is clear that it is marriage, and marriage alone, which can be the key to the whole matter. The real answer to every question of sexual behaviour can be found only when we ask how it will affect marriage. Before we can say of this or that action that it is 'right' or 'wrong' we must examine its ultimate effect upon marriage. Either on the marriage—or possible marriage—of the person asking the question; on the marriage of his or her partner in the problem; or of marriage in general as a social institution. It is on the answer to this prime question that we shall in the end make a judgement of rightness or wrongness, and we shall also almost certainly find that Christian ethics and morality will in the end take the same view.

Miss Dorothy L. Sayers in her book *The Mind of the Maker* gave a very effective answer to the people who think that the Christian commands, whether about sex or about morality in general, are completely arbitrary and capricious.

There are many people who regard God as a sort of heavenly sergeant-major or dictator whose 'rules for the nursery' we have fortunately outgrown. 'Capricious' and 'repressive' are the charges levelled at the Christian code. So she asks us to imagine that some arbitrary authority had issued a decree that no one was to cook an omelette unless they were at the same time wearing a top-hat. That would be, she says, in the highest sense arbitrary and capricious; it would be nothing but the whim of a mad dictator.

But suppose they had issued a directive that no one was to cook an omelette without first breaking eggs. That would be quite different, for, while equally the decree of an arbitrary authority, it is completely rational and sensible. Rational because it is of the nature of omelettes to be made with broken eggs. Why then bother to issue a law about it? For a vitally important reason—which those who remember war-time meals will appreciate only too easily—*to protect the general public from spurious imitations, from nasty ersatz egg-powders and similar abominations.*

Now the relation between what Christianity says are the commands of God on sex, and what common sense, looking at the whole thing from the point of view of marriage, would suggest, is remarkably like this. God has given us commands, but they happen to fit in with the way in which human nature works best. If we keep these commands then we shall be protected from wasting our time, our energy, our personality on the many spurious and *ersatz* satisfactions which sex is always suggesting to us. Marriage is the only genuine omelette, and sex, romance and love are its ingredients. They must not be turned into snacks on the way or all that will be left for the omelette may well be egg-powder.

This is perhaps why the question of the approach to marriage is almost as important as the question of marriage itself. Our life before marriage may well determine the quality of the marriage. There are three chief factors to be thought about in the question of the approach towards marriage. First there is the question of how to know and recognize genuine love. Secondly there is the question of the case for chastity before marriage. And thirdly the question of behaviour between courting or engaged persons. And they all revolve, as we said, around the real nature of marriage and of what we hope to be able to find in, and make out of, marriage—if and when it should come.

If there is one question more than any other which is asked by young people it is how to tell when love is genuine and real. And in one sense there is no answer at all. Love cannot be described, and no one has yet found a fool-proof method of sorting out the genuine article. The reason for this ought to be obvious, of course. *Real love only proves itself after a very long period*; it cannot therefore be completely and accurately pronounced upon, with no possibility of error, in that initial stage when it has not as yet grown to any stature, *and* also when it may look remarkably like something else, or rather when something else may look remarkably like it. For love has a 'terrible twin-brother', and his name is infatuation. In the initial stages the two are very alike, and only two things will in fact ever help us to sort them out. *One is time*; for infatuation never lasts. That is the terrible danger of hasty marriages, that if it was *only* infatuation it will all die out within a few months—not only die out but perhaps do what infatuation so often does when it passes; turn to active dislike. No one will deny that there have been some cases of 'love at first sight', followed by marriage within perhaps a few days, which have turned out remarkably successful. There are; but they are the exceptions which prove the rule, and the people who made them were either remarkably clear-headed, or were given a full measure of the grace of God, or both. Infatuation will not last; it is wise therefore to give any apparent affair some time to show its true colours. *The second is reason.* We all talk as if people in love took flight from reason. But if they really do this, it cannot be genuine love. For real love is always an affair of the whole personality; and that must imply using one's reason. If one may be forgiven an Irishism, one might well say two opposite things to any adolescent who asks the eternal question about knowing when love is genuine, 'You will always know when the real thing does come along', and 'Don't think you are in love the first time you think you are.' We shall know whether love is genuine or not provided we take time, use our reason, and see that the whole of our personality is involved. It is here of course that sex and glamour play us false so easily. Sex desires are strong, and their very strength may deceive us. Glamour is so attractive, so naturally and properly desirable in itself, and above all so thrown at us by the modern world, that we forget that it is the person behind the glamour with whom we have to live. Leslie Tizard in his book *Guide to Marriage* gave the perfect piece of advice on this matter. The book was written in the form of letters to a young man, and he told the young man to ask himself this sort of thing, 'You love her now. But can you imagine that you will love her when she has no make-up on, when her hair is untidy, and when the baby is being sick all over her? ' One might add, for the benefit of any girls who ask the same question, 'Can you imagine that you will love him when he is bleary and unshaven on "the morning after"? ' But that is it exactly. Do you know, so far as you can know anything, that love will be there just as strongly when all the glamour is absent? If so, then your love is probably genuine.

But isn't there an element in love that is quite beyond and behind reason? Of course there is, but what is it? We must be careful here or again we shall be shot off on a merely emotional side-track. There must be romantic and indeed erotic emotion in love, there must be sex desire also. But there must also be mental and spiritual attraction and companionship: *companionship, not identity; complement, not similarity.* There must be interests in common, but a too close correspondence in character may not be a sign of genuine love. For the transcendental part of falling in love is really a dim and only half-conscious realization of the truth of all that we have already said about the image of God being found in two different beings who yet can fuse into one. Unless the person I fancy myself in love with is genuinely my 'complement', that is, has elements in her character which I both lack and need, then my feelings are far more likely to be mere superficial glamour or infatuation. But if and when I see her, and in the shock of falling in love can only cry out, 'Without you I cannot be myself', then my reason can tell me that this thing so far beyond reason *is* genuine. *It can tell me that it is a genuinely possible starting point for that far greater love that can grow out of the twy-nature of married life together. And more than that no one can say.*

The Christian religion says that sexual intercourse between unmarried people is wrong. (It calls it by the ugly name of 'fornication'. While no one likes that word or uses it to-day, we want to remember that calling a thing by a more pleasant name does not alter its reality.) Why is it wrong?

First there is always the danger of pregnancy. Many people try to dismiss this, but the number of illegitimate babies that continue to arrive suggests that we just cannot do this. *No present method of contraception is one hundred per cent effective.* Some people even suggest that the emotional state of the parties, when unmarried, is peculiarly fostering to fertility. It is doubtful if there is any medical evidence for this—except for the undoubted fact that the fertility rate drops off very quickly after the age of about twenty-four or twenty-five—but the way in which so many people have babies when they don't want them, and so many married people can't have those they do want, should at any rate make people pause. For the unwanted baby is always a tragedy; a tragedy with incalculable personal effects upon three people. The mother, the child itself, and also, though less obviously, the father. Where unmarried people have coitus there is *always* at least an element of risk.

Secondly, and applying particularly perhaps to men, is the question of *habit*. There is many a man who 'sows his wild oats', as we say, but who says, with every sign and intention of sincerity, that, when he marries and settles down, there will be no more of that. But habits persist, and a habit of variety may well come back and hit him years after, especially when his marriage is going through the dry and trying periods that come to all marriages. When he begins to take his wife for granted, when he begins to get used to her, then the desire for that variety which he once enjoyed with apparent impunity will come back and hit him with tremendous force. And this may be almost irresistible.

Then there is memory, and especially sub-conscious memory. A man or a woman who has had sexual intercourse before marriage is usually regretful of the fact. They wish it hadn't happened, and it may well be that the whole thing has what can only be called a 'nasty taste in the mind'. Then with the wished-for and longed-for marriage there comes the act of married coitus. Exactly the same actions are going to be done again. How easily memory may come back, called up it may be by the most trivial matter, and it may very easily bring this nasty taste into the new relationship now being established.

And then there is *suspicion*. It takes time for this to arise; there will be no doubts in the honeymoon period. But later? When again the marriage is going through a trying period, the nagging suspicion of the other may begin to arise. 'I know what he was like before he married. I wonder what he is doing now with that attractive little typist.' There may be absolutely nothing at all in such a suggestion; it doesn't have to be true to generate explosive trouble. The mere suspicion, founded on known—or even guessed-at—previous behaviour may well be enough.

The modern frankness about sex is on the whole a very good thing. But there is one danger at least of which we are not always as aware as we should be. That is the danger of removing, or trying to remove, from sex and love the element of mystery. Heaven forbid that we should ever go back to the conventions and ideas of Victorian prudery; the supposed nastiness of sex has probably been removed for ever. But it is, or should be, perfectly possible to be frank about something and yet acknowledge that it is a mystery that should be approached with reverence. How many marriages have started off on the wrong foot just because the two parties came to the marriage with nothing—on the sexual side at least—to learn? Because there was no mystery to discover together, one of the greatest mutual adventures was missing. It is all tied up with what we thought about at the very beginning, the very fact that men and women are crude and rude about sex only hides what they know by instinct is a mystery. And a mystery it ought to remain for lovers to discover, and in this discovering to fertilize their love. *Unchastity tears the veil away, leaving nothing to be disclosed.*

It is this thought of the mystery reserved for marriage that will lead us on to the last consideration. Communication between persons is normally by speech or writing, but we all know that in silence there can be a communication that is even deeper than speech can possibly be. The trite expression that 'actions speak louder than words' illuminates not only the necessity of wedding actions to protestations, but the far more important fact that actions themselves can be the most powerful of all means of communication. Above all, intimate actions that, by their very intimacy, are charged with personality. Back again to the rapture of the first kiss and its meaning of ' she let me kiss her ';[1] it is the *me* and the *her* that give value and meaning to the slight sexual stimulation of lip meeting lip. And indeed so strangely again are we made that, unless actions of this kind have a personal meaning, they do not get charged with even the physical thrill that is possible to them. One might even attempt to make a sort of table of progressive meanings that attach themselves to a series of intimate personal actions such as holding hands, caressing, mild kissing and passionate kissing. It sounds very cold-blooded in print, but everyone knows the experience. But the point we are really after is this, that of all such meaningful actions, sexual intercourse is the most meaningful, because it is the *ne plus ultra* of such actions. Once you have done that you can never go any further; the ultimate act carries with it therefore the ultimate meaning. And this meaning is not just put into it by the person who performs the act, *it is essentially attached to the act by its own very nature.* All the person can do is to acquiesce in the meaning . . . or to try to wriggle out of it! Coitus of its own nature means something like, ' I am yours utterly and completely. Because I can never do anything more intimate than this with anyone, I am yours in the most intimate possible union.' That is what sexual intercourse means; and, try to get out of it as we may, to do it and not to mean this is finally to betray two personalities.

Now the most intimate and lasting union possible is that of marriage, for marriage is a taking on of both permanence and exclusiveness. Only therefore within this double bond of marriage can sexual intercourse be free to express and to symbolize its own real meaning. To have coitus with someone

[1] See p. 23.

C

other than one's spouse is in a real sense a betrayal of something that belongs, can only belong, to one's spouse. To quote Dr. Gilbert Russell again, ' A man's sexuality belongs to his wife, long before he has met her. If he *never* meets her, it belongs to nobody else. Only one human being has a claim on our sexual powers—the one who can claim the whole of us '.[1]

Only to the person who can claim the whole of us can we give such a complete commitment, and only exclusive sexual intercourse can rightly symbolize and interpret such total commitment.

There are many who would cheerfully agree with all this, but who would yet claim that such a meaningful act of commitment can perfectly properly be given before marriage by those couples who really and sincerely intend to enter into the state of matrimony. People who are deeply in love often argue in this way. ' Nothing ', they say, ' can ever unite us closer than we are now '. To talk like that is perhaps perfectly natural, indeed if they did not feel like that one would beg leave to doubt the reality of their love.

Nevertheless they are wrong. They are falling into the old, old mistake of concentrating on the birth of love as if it were the whole. We have given reasons enough for believing that love is rather like a personality, that it is born and grows, and that its full growth lasts a lifetime. The birth, like all births, is a shattering miracle, and the emotion of this is apt to overwhelm us all. But it is only a birth after all, and, if the subsequent marriage goes as it should, then the years will prove that there can come a union beside which the first rapturous emotions are as a puling baby to a full-grown man. Something more in fact *can* unite the lovers; but it is something

---

[1] *Men and Women*, pp. 65-6. We must assume that, as with our own words on p. 50, Dr Russell is not begging the question of second marriage after widowhood.

which is only made out of years of married life together, and it is made partly at least out of exclusive sexual intercourse.

But there is another thing which can unite any pair of lovers more closely after marriage than before. That is just the fact of marriage itself, which is made out of being married and not just by being in love. It may well be that they will not *feel* any more united a few days after the wedding than they did a few days before. Nevertheless something vital has happened at the wedding. Marriage has in fact united them in a way that they were not united before, with bonds that are legal and social and ecclesiastical. Whatever they may feel, they have in fact entered into a new relationship with each other. The very fact that they may not have any emotional recognition of this makes it all the more necessary that there should be some other and more factual symbol of this new relationship between them. Which is precisely what coitus, with its joint exploration of the mystery of each other's being, is meant to be. To have sexual intercourse before marriage is going to mean that marriage will pass over them with no climactic act to mark its importance and significance. This loss, unmarked perhaps at the time, may have a serious effect later on if the marriage gets thrown into the melting-pot by one of the innumerable crises which haunt every human marriage.

It is here perhaps that we should go into what is known as 'trial marriage'. There are a number of young people who have a very real sense of the importance and seriousness of marriage, and a grasp of its many possible difficulties. They might spurn the actual language of the Anglican Prayer Book, but they have imbibed very strongly the idea there set forth that marriage 'is not to be enterprised nor taken in hand unadvisedly, lightly or wantonly'. It is a serious business and therefore requires serious consideration and thought. No one would buy a suit of clothes without trying them on first, and marriage is far more serious than that. Ought people not to try out living together to see if they really are suited? That is the argument, and it is often put forward in all seriousness. Nevertheless it contains a fallacy; for whatever trial marriage is a trial of, *the one thing it cannot ever be is a trial of marriage.* For the essential element, the one thing that makes marriage different from every other kind of union, must be missing. This is the binding nature, the *permanence* of marriage. For in trial marriage one can always get out; it can always be ended by mutual consent. Real marriage can't. And therefore the reactions to tiffs or misunderstandings must be different in the two cases. It is one thing to put up for a while with someone you can leave fairly soon; *it is quite another thing to make the necessary adjustments for living with someone whom you can never get rid of.* But since the conditions are different, the one can never disclose what the reactions of either party would be under the other.

But there is more than that. There are those who, without advocating living together for a period of months, would nevertheless say that, since what is called 'sexual harmony' is considered to be of such importance, it would be as well to try out that side of marriage at least so as to see whether or not it is likely to be satisfactory. In spite of all the talk about it, the fact remains that sexual harmony is not an easy thing to attain. It usually needs both time and patience; few couples are able to achieve it at the beginning. Now the trial period suggested is not likely to be nearly long enough; and it is moreover bound to be extremely complicated by other factors, fear of pregnancy, secrecy, nervous tension, etc. The probable result is that sexual harmony will not be attained. The couple may then decide that they are not suited. But if only they had waited and had tried to find their sexual harmony within marriage, all might have come well in the end. A possibly happy marriage may be missed because the sexual side is tried out under the wrong circumstances.

But it *might*, on the other hand, work the opposite way. It might be that sexual harmony was achieved and was extremely satisfactory, and, on the strength of that one achievement, the couple decide that they must be suitable for each other. But there are many sides to marriage, and a little more thought on wider lines might have suggested that after all they were not ideally suited. A totally unsuitable marriage may be entered into because the trial of only one side was an unexpected success. We could really dispose of trial marriage by saying that it is a spurious answer to real problems. (But if we are going to stress its spuriousness, let us also remember the reality of the problems.)

There is one last possible result of pre-marital sexual intercourse between those who intend to get married. It might even mean that the marriage did not come off after all. There are many factors to be considered. There is the queer nature of the human male who is the eternal hunter, to whom the chase is always of more importance than the kill. Many a man who has 'got what he wants' comes to a sort of satiety and, not being as yet tied by the bonds of marriage and by the other creative factors that come into marriage, may cool off and eventually slide out of the engagement. And again there is the whole business of mutual respect, for, in spite of the frankness and ease of modern conventions, behaviour of this kind does still bring a certain sense of guilt. Even if this be rather defiantly put aside, it has a nasty habit of lurking round the corner. Moralists of course would say that this was a good thing; but it is the practical issue with which we are concerned at the moment. Such a sense of guilt may very easily mean loss of respect of one for the other; and that may well mean the beginning of the end of romantic love. We are always hearing of the unfortunate marriages that only happened because of pre-marital sexual intercourse: 'They had to get married'. We don't hear nearly as much about the marriages that have not come off because they were anticipated. Yet there are probably quite as many; and the results could be equally tragic.

At this point it might be well to pause and add a warning of a rather different kind. Some who have managed to read thus far may be tempted to think that it is almost impossible for an unchaste person ever to make a happy marriage, or that any marriage which has been anticipated is thereby heading straight for disaster. *Such an idea is of course complete nonsense.* Quite apart from the whole Christian doctrine of the forgiveness of sins, there are innumerable happy marriages which have been built over pre-marital unchastity. They have suffered this beginning, but they have gone on to triumph nevertheless. But 'suffered' is perhaps exactly the right word to use; for those whose experience has been along lines like these would themselves be probably the first to say that they wished that things had been different. They would agree that their marriages were more difficult to bring to success than perhaps they need have been. It is only sensible to avoid anything which will add unnecessarily to the difficulties of what must in any case be one of the most difficult things any person is called upon to attempt, i.e. to be one partner in a creatively successful marriage. (Being one of the most difficult things does not prevent its being also one of the most glorious.) To add to difficulties is silly; and another name for silliness is 'sin'.

For convinced and loyal Christians, of course, none of these things is the prime motive for chastity. For such people the prime motive will be quite simply the will and command of God; but we have surely given sufficiently weighty reasons for thinking that, in this as in so many other cases, the 'will of God' corresponds to what is best for us, and to what we ourselves would want if we were not half-blinded by selfish desires.

Before going on to the problems of behaviour between engaged or courting couples it might be as well to take a brief look at the very difficult subject of the right age for marriage. There cannot of course be any universal answer because people vary so greatly both in character and in circumstances. The only rough guide that could be given would be, 'old enough to be emotionally mature and to have a sense of responsibility. Young enough to have some romance left and not to be too set in your ways'. And it is the first and the last of these requirements that are of greatest importance. Unless a man or woman has grown up to emotional maturity—which of itself implies some sense of responsibility—there will always be trouble, not only from the danger of emotional adventures outside marriage, but because one of the most essential ingredients of creative mutual effort will be missing —dependability. While on the other hand, if either a man or a woman is too rigid and set in the ways of bachelorhood or spinsterhood the difficulties of adjustment to a joint life may be enormous.

Equally impossible to be dogmatic about is the other burning question of the length of the engagement. To say 'not too short and not too long' seems a surrender of advice altogether. Yet it is not so because at least it can help us to see what the point of an engagement is and what its difficulties are. The point of an engagement is *time*; time for knowing, time for testing, time for thinking, time for planning. By rejecting the idea of trial marriage we are committing ourselves to marriage without really knowing just what it will be like to live with this particular person . . . or for him or her to live with us. This is a risk that must be taken. We have seen that trial marriage does not in fact remove the risk of marriage, because it cannot reproduce the conditions of marriage. But at least the risk can be minimized by giving as much time and opportunity to getting to know each other, and to seeing and knowing each other under as many different kinds of circumstances, as possible. To see one another only on holiday or when we are 'at the top of our form' is not a real or a fair test of knowledge or compatibility. Time is needed to remove the danger of infatuation; time is needed for mutual confidences and planning for the future. But if the point of the engagement is time, the difficulty of the engagement is *tension. And the longer you have of the one the more you are bound to have of the other.* There are two tensions that are quite inevitable from an engagement. First the general upset of life because a totally new kind of life is due to begin. Single life is going to give place to married life; homes are going to be changed—and however lightly we think we are attached to our parents' home (or even to our lodgings) that is one of the most difficult and unsettling things to do. A change of quite fundamental importance is coming, but the longer it is in coming the less we can settle down where we are. Hence, and particularly for the woman, irritability, boredom and nerves. The second tension of course is sexual and emotional. No one is going to underestimate this to-day, but it is as well to remember that for some people it is the other tension that seems worse, and of course the two reinforce each other.

We have already said that trial marriage is a spurious answer to real problems, but in saying that we must realize that by ruling out pre-marital sexual intercourse we cannot help increasing the sexual tension of the engagement period. But that tension has also a positive purpose. There can be a positive value in this tension, *and in our acceptance of it.* But it would be foolish to increase it needlessly by an over-long engagement, or by behaviour which would increase it too much. And it is here that we approach one of the most difficult problems of all, one that is variously propounded in such questions as, 'How far ought we to go?' 'Where ought we to draw the line?' It is the eternal problem of what the Americans call 'petting and necking', or erotic stimulation. One of the things of course that all young people ought to know—how many tragedies would have been avoided if they had known—is this whole business of reflex actions and erogenous zones. The human female, though far slower to respond to sexual stimulus than the male, has several zones or areas of the body which respond to sexual stimulation. The male, while on the whole having only one such zone, responds very quickly. And in both male and female there are phenomena which happen quite automatically under stimulus. The normal male at least desires both to get and to give stimuli. Such a desire is a normal part of his sexual nature and, while it may need to be controlled, not to have such a desire would be to be abnormal. The problem of those who are not engaged or seriously in love is not really a very big one. Modesty, which is a natural instinct even before it is a moral command, will probably prevent any such behaviour. It ought to do so anyway, if one has any regard for the *person* of the other. Though even here the modern frankness of behaviour between the young of both sexes may bring dangers. (As regards what may be termed 'rough horse-play' the moment to stop is *when laughter stops*; that is the danger point and it is easily recognizable.)

But when there is added on to normal sexual desire the passionate emotion of romantic love, then a very different situation can arise. People who are engaged, or who fully intend to get married, are in a very highly charged state of emotional and sexual desire. They also desire, as we saw above, to have some sign of intimate communication which is denied to others. If others for instance may kiss the beloved, and it is conceivable that this may be the case, then the one true lover wants a further sign and symbol of union. All this is very natural, and so the question arises, *where to draw the line*. Now there are certain principles involved on which the question may be settled, certain things which all lovers ought to know, upon which they can settle their own individual problems, and again the easiest thing is to attempt to tabulate them.

(i) The late Canon Hugh Warner used to say that the line that has to be drawn, 'is not geographical so much as psychological', which is only another way of saying that persons are utterly different in their reactions. The strength of the sexual urge varies enormously in different people, the emotional reactions vary, and all this has to be added on to the already existing differing tempo of males and females. One of the purposes of an engagement indeed is to enable one to discover just what these differing reactions are. Each must find out how the tension works for the other, and then, remembering responsibility and charity, adapt his or her behaviour to the tension and tempo *of the other*. No one has the right to try another person too far, or to add unnecessary burdens on to them. And all this needs finding out and thinking about.

(ii) Most people would say, at first glance, that there could not be any two motives more different than the desire to give happiness or to express deep intimate love, and the desire for selfish gratification and indulgence. Yet in sexual matters at least the line between these two is extraordinarily difficult to draw; the one quite insensibly shades off into the other. That is why one needs to be so careful; for the second thing, the desire for self-gratification, inevitably means that we are using another person as a mere object of desire. And that is the worst thing we can ever do. To go in for erotic stimulation almost always means *in fact* that we are using another person as a mere 'thrill-making machine'. And the harm of this remains the same even though the other person is quite willing, and indeed anxious, to be so used. A good deal of clear thinking about the real nature of one's motives is needed here. This is, by the way, an admirable preparation for married life.

(iii) There is another important factor which few people seem to have noticed. It is pointed out very clearly in a very interesting little book which was first published in the United States.[1] The author, Professor P. A. Bertocci, who has obviously considerable experience of students and their problems, deals with the whole question of love and marriage. But he takes his start from that practice of 'petting and necking' which is apparently almost a convention of behaviour in certain youthful circles in America. We might note that he probably gains their sympathy because he does not start by condemning it out of hand. But he begins by saying that such erotic stimulation always brings what the business world calls 'diminishing returns'. This means that, if one goes so far and gets an appropriate thrill, one has to go further next time in order to get the same amount of thrill. Mere repetition will not apparently satisfy. Now if sexual intercourse is ruled out (as apparently it is in the American 'convention', and as it would be in the cases we are considering), then there comes very soon a stage when one just cannot go any further. Consequently what we may term the 'thrill potential' is diminished. Most lovers would of course hotly deny that thrill potential was their motive. But clear thinking on the lines suggested above would show that in many cases it was at least the sub-conscious motive. And in such cases the fact that the loved one has now a diminished thrill potential may have serious results.

(iv) But the most important consideration is perhaps the simplest of all, and arises from the physiological nature of

[1] *The Human Venture in Sex, Love and Marriage*, Longmans, 1957.

such stimuli as are involved in serious 'petting and neck-ing'. Because of the reflex actions on the genital organs, such stimuli are a necessary and integral part of the approach to full sexual intercourse. They ought to be done, they have to be done, before proper sexual intercourse can be effected, for this 'love-play' as it is sometimes called, *causes* the neces-sary tumescence. Such actions wind up energy as it were, energy both nervous and emotional as well as physical. If sexual intercourse follows in the normal course of events, then all this energy dies away in detumescence. It dies away naturally leaving behind it only a sense of peace and langour.

But suppose normal coitus does not follow. Then indeed the situation is different. It is as if a powerful spring had been wound up and not allowed to unwind. Detumescence will of course follow, but it will follow with a sense of conflict and frustration. And while physical detumescence will happen fairly quickly, nervous and emotional tumescence may persist for a long while—especially in the case of the woman. To go in for such stimulus and not to follow it up by coitus is in fact using something for a purpose for which it was not designed. The religious will call that 'sin'; and the practical can add that it is unwise and unkind.

If out of all this we attempt to formulate any rules, one could perhaps say that lovers should never (*a*) use another person as a mere thrill-making machine, (*b*) never go so far as would make sexual intercourse inevitable, (*c*) never go so far as would make the keeping away from sexual intercourse too much of a strain for either party. Not only must we avoid doing wrong ourselves, we have no right to im-pose on another person an intolerable strain in order that we may pride ourselves on our own chastity or self-control.

That all this will involve great self-control is obvious. It may also, for particular persons, involve not doing things which may in themselves seem to be perfectly all right. But it is a necessary discipline. The subsequent marriage will be all the better for it, but it provides a powerful reason why the engagement should not be unduly prolonged.

FIVE

The Heart of Marriage

THERE will be some readers who, seeing that this chapter is largely about sex, will think that we are falling into the very trap against which we have, at least by implication, already warned them; the trap of thinking that sex is the whole of marriage. But the real heart of marriage with which we are concerned here is—not sex, but *creativity*; the creation of full, vital personalities. This may come about of course by the biological process of procreation and conception wherein completely new personalities are born into the world. But it may also come about through that complement and fulfilment whereby two separate and incomplete persons are fused together into a larger and fuller whole; the 'twy-nature' or 'mystic third person' of marriage.

Full creativity of course includes both of these, and these are therefore the things for which marriage (and love and sex as pointers), really exists. These are the creative things that make the heart of marriage.

But both of them arise out of sex, and to discuss them must involve some discussion of sexual activity; and of the inevitable problems which arise out of this. It is very true that 'going to bed is not the whole of marriage', yet it is the creativity which is inseparable from sex which is at the heart of marriage, and so the problems and questions of ordinary sexual activity must be faced.

The first question might well be, what is the place of sex in marriage? We have answered that in theory. Sex is the catalyst which fuses together the elements of union on other levels, and, out of the whole, makes a new mixture. But it is not of this that the average bride and groom are thinking. For them there is a much more practical question. How large a place in thought, motive and actual practice, ought sexual intercourse to have in their joint married life? And the question is almost forced upon them by reason of the contradictory advice that is flying about. On the one hand there is the continual talk by clergy, and other religious-minded folk, of 'restraint', 'control' and so on. No one denies the need for these things in the Christian life, but it can very easily be made to look as if the Church were really rather afraid of sex, as if Christian opinion, while sanctioning sex, was desperately anxious not to give it its head. Against this we can quote Dr Gilbert Russell again: 'Desire is never the enemy of love because it is strong, but only when it is narrow, when it is *merely* sexual'[1]—*that is when it forgets to be creative*. But if old-fashioned religious opinion tended to play sex down, modern secular opinion is doing the opposite. Young people thinking of marriage are to-day subject to a furious bombardment of books, pamphlets, talks, etc., all of which stress the idea that sex, and one particular aspect of sex too, is the one all-important thing in their married life. It is the usual affair of good and evil being mixed up together. The modern frankness of speech and writing and the realization of the essential goodness and rightness of sex have combined together to make it possible for what one may call the 'technique of coitus' to be explained simply and accurately. And very necessary it is that all those who approach marriage should know the basic facts of such technique. But it can be overdone. The idea can easily be spread that sexual intercourse is technique and nothing else. Many brides have complained rather ruefully of their husbands as it were

[1] *Men and Women*, p. 64, my italics.

getting into bed with a handbook in one hand. But even worse than that, this emphasis on knowledge of the technique gives to what is called 'sexual harmony' a dangerously false importance. One of the specious motives, for instance, for trial marriage was to make certain that sexual harmony would be attained. We saw many reasons for condemning the practice. But not to 'try it out first' must also mean leaving it to chance; must mean taking the risk that sexual harmony may not be attained after marriage. Quite so. But there is another risk that must be taken also; that of infertility. It is well known that in some rural areas it used to be the convention that one did not marry until the girl was already pregnant. Sexual intercourse before marriage was indulged in, *not* just to satisfy desire, but to ensure that the couple could have children. If the girl did not conceive there was no wedding. And in the days when children were an economic necessity one can well understand the social pressure which lay behind such a convention. We have already condemned all pre-marital intercourse for various weighty reasons. Very good; but that will mean that infertility has to be risked. Marriage is a lottery, in fact. No one likes that term, and it certainly does not tell the ultimate truth about marriage. But it does state the truth about *one* aspect; that in marriage you have to put your hand in the bag and take what you get. And you have to risk a lot of things happening. No risk; no adventure. That is also true; but there are two risks that are quite inseparable from pre-marital chastity. One is childlessness; the other is possible failure to attain sexual harmony.

This insistence by the little books on sexual technique that sexual harmony is vital to the success of marriage is apt to frighten a good many people. This fear itself, by creating a state of quite unnecessary tension, may actually prevent the easy attainment of the harmony which is desired. There is a vicious circle here which must be broken. And the way to break it is to remember that there are very many happily married couples who have very rarely, and indeed perhaps never, managed to attain mutual sexual harmony. There are wives and mothers, happy as each, who have never had an orgasm at all. This is not the normal way of marriage, no one would call such a state of things desirable in itself, but the fact that such couples exist, and exist in happiness and real fulfilment, should help to lay the bogy that sexual harmony is the whole, or even the chief part of, marriage. The truth is that while sexual harmony is most desirable and should be sought after, slowly and gently and patiently, it is not absolutely necessary for successful marriage. It is not uniquely necessary for a happy marriage.

This modern insistence of the necessity for sexual harmony, this idea that if this fails the marriage fails too, has another and even more dangerous corollary. That is the idea that if sexual harmony is perfect, then the marriage is automatically a roaring success. Nothing could be further from the truth. We need to remember the advice of Emile Cammaerts in *For Better For Worse*, that to marry for the sake of children only is a mistake: to marry solely for the sake of sex is a disaster. For those who marry solely for the sake of sex, who marry each other primarily so that they can sleep together, will almost certainly find two terrible and perhaps unexpected things. First that when sex fades out, as it must to some extent do in every marriage, there is nothing else at all to hold them together. Secondly, the fact that where sex is regarded as the be-all and end-all of life together, it will fade out quicker than ever. It might well fade out after six months. (There have even been cases where the parties had had so much sexual activity before marriage that after getting married they never slept together at all. Such cases are extreme, but they do point out how human nature is apt to work.)

There is a terrible danger in all this over-emphasis on sex, and here it is well to remember something else. One of the most important changes in feeling and emotion that occurs during marriage is the change over *from passion to tenderness*. This comes about in various ways; and one of them is obviously from sexual harmony and mutual fulfilment. But it can also arise from disappointment at failure to attain harmony, if that disappointment be taken in the right way. We all know of couples who are childless through no fault of their own. They were 'unlucky'; the fertility risk inherent in pre-marital chastity worked for them the wrong way. This is a frustration; and not only for the woman. Yet we have also met childless couples like this between whom there reigns a harmony and tenderness superior to and deeper than that between many who have a large family. How does this come about? Surely because a disappointment shared had led to tenderness; failure on one side of marriage has not led to failure on the other sides. Rather has it led to an even greater and more self-sacrificing effort to make a success of those sides of marriage which are within their power. It may be exactly the same over lack of sexual harmony where this is not the fault of either. It is one of the most fundamental Christian doctrines that good can come out of evil. This does not mean that we are to be indifferent to what is less than the perfect *desideratum*; but it does mean that such failure can be a challenge rather than a disaster, a spur rather than a halter.

But if over-emphasis on sex is a danger, so on the other hand is under-emphasis. The husband who confessed that he thought that sexual intercourse was a 'vastly over-rated entertainment' had something seriously wrong either with his marriage or with his general outlook on life. Such under-emphasis is more common than one would think, and especially on the part of women. It springs from two things, perhaps. One is lack of knowledge about the technique of coitus, lack of understanding that there is such a thing as *mutual* orgasm, that in perfect coitus as God intended it to be, the woman should be as joyful as the man. This lack of knowledge is, as we see, being rapidly dissipated, and indeed with too much emphasis in the other direction. The other reason is more deep-seated; it springs from the remnant of puritanical ideas that are still with us. How many mothers have said to their daughters, in that last terrible five minutes of so-called marriage preparation: 'You won't enjoy it, but you must put up with it; men are like that.' The implication being that men are lustful brutes who want something that is not really nice; that a loving wife will give her husband what he wants because she loves him, but that, if he were perhaps *really nice*, he wouldn't want it, or at least would be less importunate about it! How many men also come to the sexual side of marriage with a 'nasty taste in the mind' that derives, *not* from previous experience, but from inbred ideas about all that sort of thing being 'dirty': the sort of thing one ought to mention when one confesses one's sins. The amount of harm that has been done by well-meaning clergy and ministers over this is quite incalculable. In their very proper zeal for chastity (which they persist in miscalling 'purity') they have driven deep into the minds of devout and innocent young men the idea that any sexual feelings and desires are of themselves 'impure' and nasty. One can easily imagine the mental confusion that arises when these so-called 'impure desires' are put into action with someone whom one has hitherto placed on a pedestal of unapproachable 'purity'. Sometimes indeed these deep-seated ideas implanted by unwise parents during early childhood have issued in actual impotence or frigidity. That may be rare, but a frustration caused by under-emphasis on the creative role of sex in the one-flesh-union is all too common.

Sex is creative; it creates the one-flesh-union of the 'mystic third person', and it creates children and a family. *The two sides of its creativeness are, where fertility is possible, quite inseparable.* We say quite clearly that, from a Christian point of view, *to marry and then deliberately to refrain from having any children at all, when it is possible and safe to have them, is and must be wrong.* It might be as well to go into the reasons for this firm statement. Childless marriages are bound to be more difficult than fertile ones. We have seen that involuntary childlessness is a frustration that can be turned to good account. But it remains a frustration all the same, and such marriages do labour under special difficulties. It must be wrong then to lay, either upon oneself, or still more upon another, a completely needless and unnecessary burden. Marriage is always difficult; to make it more so must be wrong.

The difficulties and frustrations of childlessness, either deliberate or involuntary, come from the very nature of human beings and of the common life of husband and wife which they are making out of their marriage. We said that woman is meant to have as much enjoyment out of coitus as man. That is so, but it also remains true that for a woman coitus is never an end in itself (as it at any rate seems to be to men) it is only one stage in a whole cycle of life, to which her whole nature, physical and emotional and psychological, is attuned. This cycle is coitus, conception, parturition, weaning and motherhood. It all goes together, and complete personal fulfilment, even though by no means always attained in particular cases, is only possible through the whole cycle. To some extent also the same is actually true of the man. He may not be so conscious of the desire for fatherhood, especially before marriage. But after marriage it is different; if fatherhood is not attained then, there is a frustration which often rises indeed into the consciousness. And even if it does not, an unconscious frustration can do an awful amount of harm.

In marriage husband and wife set out to attain a common life through community, but community is incomplete if it does not issue in its natural and normal widening into a family.

Finally of course there is the direct command of the Almighty. We may perhaps look rather differently on the old Genesis myths from the way our ancestors did; but all the same the command 'be fruitful and multiply' is implied in every doctrine and thought which sees God as above all the Creator and the Source of Life. We have discussed at some length the higher meaning and purpose of the sexual division amongst mankind; yet, as we also said, sex remains sex all through. We are in fact all born with half the machinery for reproducing life and with a strong desire to mate with someone of the other half; and this fact of human nature means that procreation is the scheme of God. And as such it cannot by married persons be completely denied without sin.

Children if possible; yes. But at once we are plunged into the question of Family Planning, and this is something to which a good deal of thought must be given, before marriage, surely, as well as after.

No Christian of any school of thought to-day would surely suggest that because 'God sends children', husband and wife should give no thought at all as to their number or times of arrival; but should have coitus as often as they desire it and leave the results entirely to what 'God' or 'nature' sends. To do this, at least without thought, seems to be abdicating some of the principal things which distinguish men from animals: reason, foresight, the power to control events (within limits of course) and the proper acceptance of responsibility for actions which these other powers imply. If the procreation of children be in fact one of the highest possible functions of humanity, an act in which man most nearly approaches to his Creator, and also an act fraught with incalculable results for all parties concerned, then it would seem to be the grossest betrayal to allow such a thing to happen with no foresight, planning or intention at all. There are of course innumerable other reasons, such as the health of both mother and children, the happiness and prosperity of the family, which suggest that no Christian couple ought to do other than take the utmost thought to the matter of the number and spacing of their hoped-for family.

A great many people get married with two firm intentions. One is to have a family; the other is *not to start a family for two or three years*. Indeed this custom is now so widespread that, quite apart from the controversy over the morality of artificial contraception, it is worth going into. One of the reasons often given is that, as we have said almost *ad nauseam*, sexual harmony takes time to achieve, and pregnancy may interfere with this. But such a suggestion overlooks the fact that the difficulties of sexual harmony are more often psychological than purely physical. Over-anxiety about it will itself hinder it. But one of the really determining factors against achieving sexual harmony is, as Dr Gilbert Russell suggests, the ' grasping ego ' of one or other. *Parenthood may well subdue this* quicker than anything. That is why he says very firmly that in trying to weigh up the value of achievement of sexual harmony with the value of having a child as early as possible, we may well be making a completely false distinction. Early parenthood may help towards sexual harmony rather than hinder it.

But there are two other powerful considerations that must not be forgotten. The first is the physical fact that the fertility rate drops off very rapidly after about the age of twenty-five. The other is psychological, and it concerns what the modern jargon would call the ' pattern of living '. The big change that marriage brings of course is the change from the pattern of single life to the pattern of double life. But with the arrival of the first child the pattern of ' life-as-two ' must give way to the pattern of ' life-as-three—or four, or more? Now the change from the pattern of ' life-as-two ' to that of ' life-as-three ' is a difficult one. It is moreover a change to a pattern that is, in all human probability, going to last a great deal longer. In a marriage of normal fertility the ' life-as-two ' period is very short compared to the ' life-as-family '. Would it not be a good thing then to get into the larger and more permanent pattern as soon as possible? But just as an individual may tend to cling to the pattern of single life through selfishness, so a couple may tend through selfishness to cling to the double pattern and be unwilling to go on. Again, just as the longer one is a bachelor or spinster the more difficult are the adjustments necessary for double-harness, *so the longer the pattern of two goes on the more difficult will be the transition to the pattern of three.* Any couple who have had to wait for some years for a child will say that, great though the joy of the child was, the difficulty of changing the whole pattern of life accepted over the years, was enormous. The sooner the inevitable change is accepted, the easier will the transition be.

Granted that a family is both desirable and possible, the inevitable question arises of ' How many? ' This of course no one can answer for anyone else, it depends so entirely upon circumstances. Most would agree however that a single child is to be avoided if at all possible. No doubt some psychologists enormously exaggerate the harm of being an only child; but that it does make for a difficult adjustment to life and opens the door to all sorts of emotional troubles, for the parents as well as for the child, is quite undeniable. No couple should, unless it be unavoidable, *condemn either themselves or their offspring to the difficulties of a one-child family.*

But what number of children really constitutes a family, a family in the sense of a really creative and fertile community? (For it is as a community which is the seed-bed of personality that the family exists.) Or, that being answered, how many children is it wise to have in this difficult modern world? Dr Gilbert Russell has some very wise words here about the all-too common objection that ' we just can't have more than two '.

'Most families are now too small to function *as families*; to perform their specific task for each of their members. " Quality not quantity " is a dangerous slogan when applied to human breeding. It has lent support to prodigious rationalization of parents' motives. It is obvious that the one- or two-child family can often secure for its offspring certain advantages which cannot well be shared among four or five. Education is an example. The parents may just afford to send an only child to a first-rate school; if he had brothers and sisters, none of the children could go to it. Undue concern about clothes and inordinate care for appearances may set a false standard of living which adds to the family budget what would pay for another baby, or more than one.

. . . No substitute exists for that which four or five children mean to each other and to the family group. The " best chance " a child can have is that which brothers and sisters, and no one else, can provide.'[1]

The operative words here of course are ' false standards of living '; while the other idea could be put most simply by posing a query. When you have one baby already, *which is the better thing for that existing child*; to have a T.V. set so that it can look at Bill and Ben, the Flower-pot Men, or to have

[1] *Men and Women*, pp. 89-90.

a brother or sister? Put like that there is only one answer, but of course we all know that the matter is never quite so simple. Yet Christians will surely agree that these 'false standards of living' are the real bane of modern society over every field of life, and that it is by now a Christian duty to oppose them, and sometimes to act and live in defiance of them. And this comes deeply into the planning of a family.

But granted that both limiting the number and spacing the arrival of children is a duty in most cases, we are brought up against the problem of how this is to be accommodated to the sexual desires of normal people. Indeed the question is much more than just one of *desire*; the important place which sex holds in the whole marriage relationship demands that we must face this accommodation. There are two periods of married life in which some such accommodation may be necessary. After one has what is honestly considered to be the largest number of children that one ought to have; and the time between the birth of the last child and the desired conception of the next.

And it is here that we face the question of artificial contraception, which is fundamentally a religious and moral question. The fact that contraceptives are available for all and sundry, and the fact that they are used by a vast number of people, *do not of themselves mean that their use is either right or morally justified*. It may be, but it must be argued on grounds other than either convenience or mere common acceptance of their use.

We must not forget that many Christians hold very strong views against them, and, though we may not agree with them, we ought in all fairness to try and see why they do object. Christian couples who belong to any Christian Church will no doubt consider carefully what their particular Church has to say in the matter. Whatever others, other Christians even, may think, membership of a Church implies loyalty to that Church's moral commands.

What is the present position? The Roman Catholic Church in its official moral teaching at present condemns artificial contraception absolutely. It does allow, under proper circumstances however, the use of what is called the 'safe period' (see below). The Church of England has no official teaching as such on the matter. The same is true of course of the Free Churches. Some clergy and ministers feel as the Romans do; others think that contraception is a normal part of married life when one has fulfilled one's responsibilities; others again feel that contraception can never be an ideal, but that there are many circumstances when any other course would result in definite harm of some kind. It is to be noted that all Christian teachers would hold that the use of contraceptives to avoid responsibility is always wrong; and that is a pretty large measure of agreement.

There are two methods of avoiding conception which may be dismissed in a few words. Abstention from coitus is of course the only absolutely fool-proof method; but, unless a couple were completely convinced in their own consciences that this is what God wished them to do, it would not be advised for the reason that it cuts out the other side of the creativity of coitus. The practice known as *coitus interruptus* must be unhesitatingly condemned on all grounds.

Something must however be said about the 'safe period' because, quite apart from its value as a contraceptive practice, it has very important moral considerations over the whole matter of sex. It should properly be called, not the 'safe period', for indeed it is not completely 'safe', but the 'period of minimum fertility'. This is precisely what it is; and we must see how it works. It is now generally accepted that the normal human female has a cycle of ovulation, *and that there is an ovum present to be fertilized for only four or five days out of the whole menstrual cycle.* It is also a fact that, normally again, male sperms cannot remain active inside a human body for more than a few days at the very outside. Calculations therefore ought to be able to show that there are lengthy periods when conception *could not result from coitus.*

That is theory; but unfortunately human beings are not machines, and theory is apt to be upset by other factors and circumstances. The 'safe period' is not safe completely. (Nor on the other hand are contraceptives. Research carried out recently suggests that the percentage of 'failures' of contraceptives on the one hand, and of the use of the 'safe period' or of *coitus interruptus* on the other, was about equal.)

This period of minimum fertility is thus not an absolute bar against fertility; but surely any Christian couple who felt that this was the way in which God was calling them to adjust their desires and their foresight would be content to leave the result in His hands. If God calls us to use a method that is uncertain, then surely we must believe that 'the Lord will provide'. Do we not all know of innumerable cases of the child whose birth was an 'accident' turning out to be the most loved of all?

What are the reasons, however, why many Christians think that the use of artificial contraceptives is wrong? They are probably two. First that they are an interference with nature. The reply to that is easy; so is all surgery and a good deal of medicine also. But there is an equally telling reply to that. Surgery interferes with nature only with the object of saving life or prolonging it. Contraception interferes with the object of preventing new life arising. Its use therefore involves a moral choice.

But the strongest argument, and the one that lies behind all the others is this. *Contraception is said to be a deliberate interference with the natural and God-intended purpose of the act of coitus, an interference solely in the interests of personal pleasure.*

For many Christians this is enough and the question settles itself. But, with all due respect to the teachers and theologians who hold such views, one ventures to suggest two things. First, this is an over-simplification; and secondly, it takes for granted something which is at the very least open to considerable argument.

It is an over-simplification to suggest that the motive for having sexual intercourse without pregnancy following is always that of purely personal pleasure. Of course personal pleasure is involved; God made us with nerves and feelings that work that way. But a couple who really understand the place of sex in marriage will wish to make love for a much deeper reason than that. They know that coitus is the sacramental act by which they not only realize, but actually make, their mutual unity. Even their conscious motive may well be the forging of that union of two in one which is both the image of God and the highest possibility for human personality.

Again we may ask whether conception is the 'natural and God-intended purpose of *every* act of coitus'. Not only are there certain times—after the menopause and with sterile couples—when we may be certain it will not follow; but our whole understanding of the 'period of minimum fertility' tells us that there are lengthy periods when conception is very unlikely. Indeed the truth is that, even at periods of maximum fertility, *we can never be certain* that conception will result. The truth surely could best be expressed thus:

> '*Conception is the normal and natural, and therefore God-intended, result of a number of acts of coitus. It is not the natural and inevitable result of every such act.*'

It seems difficult therefore to suggest that it is the purpose of every act. On the other hand this mutual unity of husband and wife *can be a result of every act of coitus.*

Rigid opponents of contraception seem here to be making a wrong distinction. They distinguish between procreation and pleasure. Making all allowances for the fact that many men and women are self-indulgent over sex, the true division is rather between the two creative purposes of sex; the procreational and the unitive. Granted that it is wrong to make a *permanent* separation between these two, by deliberately refraining from having children when one can, the question is; Is a temporary separation always to be condemned? Especially when nature itself makes such a separation without either our knowledge or our will on so many occasions?

It is at this stage that the modern Christian teacher would probably prefer to leave the matter. It is something that every couple must make up their own minds about, having regard to their own beliefs and their own circumstances. But they must make up their minds with both prayer and intelligence. To say either 'Oh, it's all wrong' on the one hand, or 'It must be all right, everyone does it' on the other, is to slide away from the moral issues involved. The thing that really matters is, not so much what any couple actually do, as to why they do it; whether or not they have used thought and prayer and placed the glory of God in their lives first.

SIX

The Aftermath

'A N D so they lived happily ever after. . . .'; the fairy-tale ending to the story that everyone covets for their own. And it happens to come true far more often than we probably realize. But not automatically; it is never one of those things that just happen. For real happiness in marriage, as in everything else, is always a result, almost a by-product. It springs from a real creative effort of will, an effort which usually involves both doing and suffering a great many things we don't either like or wish for, or wouldn't wish for unless we were urged on by love, of course. That may be true; but it is also true that love, regarded as a red-hot emotional urge, is apt to fade away—or at least mysteriously transform itself into something else. It is the inevitability of these changes which forces us to realize that the most important part of any marriage can only be what comes after; the aftermath. It is the most important part not just of any marriage, but of any genuine love-affair.

We have already laboured that false picture of love which the cinema and the more vapid of the women's magazines are apt to thrust down our throats. It is a false picture in the most dangerous sense of all; that of telling a large part of the truth. Glamour *is* important, sex emotions are right and proper; desire, thrill and romance all have their part to play. We are all moved by these, we ought to be moved by them. But they are not the whole of love; and that is the danger, that we may mistake the part for the whole, and so for ever

miss that wholeness we might have had. But there is something even more false about the picture so often given. The
'cinema mentality' has one grand assumption, which it
almost hypnotizes us into accepting without question; this
is the assumption that what we call 'romantic love' ends with
marriage. In ninety-nine films out of a hundred the fade-out
shews the lovers in each other's arms. Now they will get
married; we take that for granted. But we also take it for
granted that the exciting part of the story is now over. What
follows, so we are made to think, is not so much an aftermath
as an anti-climax. There is only one occasion in which
'romantic glamorous love' is allowed to appear after
marriage; and that is when it is love with a third party. That
this makes for a good story is undeniable, as is also the fact
that it happens all too frequently in real life. It is a problem
we shall have to face, but to suggest that this is all that is left
for real love after marriage is to miss the essential meaning
of both love itself and also of marriage.

So far from starting to die from the moment that passionate
lovers get married, their love ought really to be only beginning
a new and adult kind of life. How often have lovers used semi-
religious language to try and describe what has happened to
them? They felt 'born again', 'converted into a new kind of
world'. That there is a real religious significance in the
experience of love is not to be denied, but these phrases
suggest a more familiar but equally striking kind of metaphor.
For we have already likened the crisis of falling in love to
that other crisis in the life of the individual wherein he is
shot out into a new and unfamiliar world at physical birth.
'Falling in love' is, in a real sense, being born again; but
if falling in love is like birth, *getting married is like coming
of age*. A child exists from birth, and love exists from the
moment of crisis; but it exists privately and, in no bad sense,
irresponsibly. Getting married does for love precisely what

coming of age does for the adolescent. It gives public, legal, and social recognition not merely of his existence, but of his status and responsibility. If birth be the beginning of life, then this is the beginning of adult life. And just as the most important parts of the life of normal individuals are the long years of adult life that follow coming of age, so the really important and creative part of any love affair that goes the right way is the adult responsible life that follows marriage. For it is only in those years that love can attain its maturity. The situations are almost exactly parallel, and we would all see it if we were not so bewildered and bamboozled into concentration on the emotional crisis of the birth of the affair.

Think for a moment of any couple we know. We can see them growing up as separate individuals, becoming conscious of sex, finding the strange and disturbing fascination of the opposite sex, flirting a little and 'trying their wings', looking for some satisfaction they cannot define—and then suddenly finding each other, precipitated now into the possibility of a new kind of life altogether. But instead of wasting pages on the story of how they came to fall in love, we ought to hurry on. Love has come; now, for each of them, the only real life is imagined in terms of a joint life together. And so they get married; they enter into the state of matrimony, and their love enters into its fully adult phase. *And at once it begins to settle down . . .* for that is a sign of real maturity. (It must do this; any couple who remained in the 'billing and cooing' stage proper to the engagement period would be heading straight for a nervous breakdown or would be showing serious signs of psychological immaturity.) But 'settling down' always means the same thing. *It means passing from reliance on the emotions to reliance on the determination and the will.* It must therefore mean a change in both the direction and the tempo of the emotions. 'Passion must turn into tenderness'.

That is quite right, but we must not overlook the fact that this also means some diminution at least of 'glamour'. And if 'glamour' is all that we sought, then we shall hate and resent, and indeed fight, its going. Half the trouble in marriage arises from the resistance put up by one party or the other to the inevitable changes involved in the growing and maturing of that very love which originally called them together.

And it is round about this stage too that the family will normally begin to appear. And the appearance of a family, like any other shattering event, is both a crisis and a challenge. It is all very well to talk sentimentally about 'little fingers binding the parents together'. It does not by any means always work out that way, and it won't ever work out like that without considerable effort. Parenthood may be fulfilment both biological and psychological, but there is no denying that it is also a vast increase of that *limitation* which was one of the first rules of the game of marriage, and the hardest to adapt oneself to. The coming of a family means not only increased limitation, it also inevitably means increased *irritation*. This may seem a small point, but it is the little things— the mess of nappies, the weariness, the restriction of social life—that mount up. If accepting limitation be the first rule of married life, a second could well be: 'beware of making mountains out of molehills!'

For this is precisely what everyone tends to do. It is not only a matter of the extra irritation (balanced of course by a new joy and responsibility) of children; it comes close into the relationship of husband and wife. For with the ending of the 'honeymoon period' of glamour, husband and wife begin at last to face each other as *real persons*. Adjustment has got to be made, not to the vision, but to the reality; *and no reality of another person is altogether acceptable to the 'grasping ego' of any of us.* It is far more often the trivial

D

things that annoy us than the real faults of character. Many a husband cheerfully puts up with the fact that his wife is a bad manager or has no money sense, and is driven to fury by her habit of sniffing. Many a woman who will forgive her husband's real weaknesses just cannot stand his eternal talk about cricket or the pools. But both have got to be dealt with, the trivial and the serious, both have got somehow to be accepted and worked into the common pattern. They can be, but the process is not easy, *and the emotions may be pulling the wrong way all the time.*

No two marriages go the same way any more than two individuals are identical; yet there is a certain pattern into which most marriages tend to fall. There will always be crises, big or little, of some kind, but there are two special crises which are so common that something ought to be said about them. The first is this 'outside affair' already referred to; and the second is what some would call the actual death of love within the marriage itself.

The outside affair may vary enormously in its seriousness. It may be nothing more than a mild flirtation that is in itself perfectly harmless, but to which the other partner objects. It may be a passionate love affair in which the spouse concerned thinks that the marriage was a fatal mistake because the only love of a life-time has now appeared.

We might start by asking the question of how far it is wise for husbands and wives to have close friends of the opposite sex. How far, for instance, is it wise to keep up with previous 'flames'? Most of us would suggest that this is likely to prove a risky proceeding in all circumstances. But, allowing for that, are husbands and wives to be deprived of the friendship, the sympathy, the interests and the culture, of persons of the opposite sex, just because they are of the opposite sex? The very fact that husbands and wives are complementary in character means that there will always be some cultural or

other interests which they do *not* share. No one expects a wife
to be deeply interested in golf or cricket; and the husband may
have his male friends to share these interests. But suppose he
is interested also in music and the wife is not? Must his
musical friends be as male as his sporting friends? Is there
any logical reason why husbands and wives should confine
their friends to the same sex? Is such a limitation fair to
the ideals of partnership and freedom which most couples
hold; is it fair to the trust that should be between them
to make such a restriction? Yet, if friendships are not so
limited, there will always be danger. Of course there will;
just as there will be danger of a different kind by making too
much of the idea of limitation. The only comment one can
make on this, as on so many other aspects of marriage, is to
repeat the saying: 'every marriage walks along a knife-edge;
and success lies in not falling over the edge'. The late Charles
Williams in his great book *The Figure of Beatrice* has some
very strong words to say about the terrible effects of the sin
of jealousy. This grasping and hugging to oneself of that
which belongs only to God has ruined far more individuals
and far more marriages than ever adultery has. If
only, he says, the Church had thundered against this
as she has thundered against adultery, how much
more we might be able to understand the real nature of
marriage.

There is always danger, and every couple must face and
brave these dangers in their own way, but a piece of practical
advice would be to suggest that most of the dangers would be
minimized or guarded against if only the friend of the opposite
sex is, or is made into, *a friend of both*.

The more superficial outside affairs, especially when they go
so far as to involve actual unfaithfulness, probably happen
to, or are indulged in, by men more frequently than women.
And it is here that women need to have a proper understand-

ing of the essential sexual differences between male and female human nature. Man is essentially the hunter; that is his biological function, to seek out the female and impregnate her. This is a quick, temporary, and, to all appearances, a superficial matter. That it is not really superficial we have already seen; but this essentially different function on the biological plane does mean that there are two aspects of male sexuality that are quite foreign to the female. One is the quickness of response and stimulus, and the other is the fact that a man tends to *think of* sex primarily in terms of its 'entertainment value', its emotional value. It does not have for him, in his conscious thoughts, the same depth of 'personality-value' that it must have for the woman. The result is all too easy to see. A man wants emotional comfort, and he naturally seeks this in a woman. His easily aroused sexual nature will turn this into a desire for coitus almost before he realizes it. And he can very easily turn the desire into action without any intention at all of deep personal union. There must be many husbands who have fallen into tragedy by thus being unfaithful to their wives 'almost by accident'. They never intended for one moment to leave or desert their wives, they continued to love them (and love them quite genuinely too), but their essentially male response to stimulus made them fall into adultery almost before they knew where they were.

Women must learn to understand men. Even the most rigid and moral of men is still a man. His eyes, at least, can never quite keep from straying, and this, not because he is 'naughty', but because he is a male. A man can be unfaithful to his wife, and that more than once, and yet still have for her a love and a tenderness that he has for no one else. He fails utterly to see that for her, with her totally different nature to which coitus is always a long-drawn-out act of deep personal commitment, this act of his is a fearful blow. Men also need to understand women, and to face the power of hurt that resides in their own essential male natures.

However, apart from questions of actual unfaithfulness, whether in thought only or in deed, there must be few marriages indeed in which the husband at least has not at some time had a sentimental quasi-emotional affair with some other woman. The old quip suggested that the danger year for marriage was the seventh . . . or was it the tenth? But there are solid reasons for suggesting that this often happens. For this is the time when two complementary and opposite things are likely to happen. First of all the original excitement of glamour-romance has either faded out or has been transformed; each now takes the other for granted. Husband and wife have become for each other part of the essential furniture of daily life. That is right and proper; the danger of course lies in being considered as no more than a piece of old furniture. The home and the family are safe and solid, the foundations are truly laid. They are therefore more able to stand shocks than they were; it is 'safer to take risks'. We forget that of course it is never safe, and therefore always a silly thing to do.

But just because, perhaps, solidity, comfort and security are now achieved and accepted, there arises at the same time the desire for variety, for a little extra excitement, a new or new-old thrill. And there is of course nearly always someone standing in the wings who is only too anxious to supply this need.

There are moreover, in the male at least, powerful psychological urges at work as middle-age approaches or is reached : the desire to recapture the lost youth, to have a last fling, to prove that 'there's life in the old dog yet'. It is not only the desire to recapture and renew the thrills and glamour we once knew, and which will all too soon become utterly unattainable because of old age; there is the virile desire to prove that we are still a man capable of attracting a female; capable of cutting out the immature youths. And this desire to prove to oneself the still existing power of attraction works perhaps even more powerfully in the female of the species. It is not necessary for any of these desires to be in the conscious mind; they will do their work just as well if they are unconscious and unrecognized urges.

But the result is all too often a sudden renewal of the silliest form of sentimental infatuation. And if the wife cannot supply the necessary amount of understanding and sympathy, then these will be sought elsewhere, and probably with fatal results. The husband must not try and fool himself that this sort of thing has not happened. Nor on the other hand ought he to nurse an unnecessary load of guilt about it. It must just be faced for what it is; a temporary infatuation which has many causes, most of which we cannot help and are not responsible for. We cannot help feeling it; *we can help submitting to it*. The first essential thing is to understand it— and this means understanding by both partners, and the third party too if possible—and then to avoid its obvious entanglements. Seeing what it is is the first step to getting over it; and the memory of ' lost youth ' which probably prompted it, should surely tell one that infatuation in fact never lasts.

But sometimes it goes very much deeper than this. There are people who, perhaps long years after marriage, fall into a desperately serious affair with someone else. It may be indeed that their marriage was not founded on romantic love at all; they mistook infatuation for the real thing, or they married on the basis of friendship only. In such a case the victim may be perfectly justified in saying that the ' love of a lifetime ' has now appeared. But much more likely, and far more disturbingly, the marriage *was* founded on a genuine romantic love-affair. And here is apparently the same thing appearing all over again. Indeed, because of its inevitable disturbance and extra emotional upset, it may well feel even more shattering than anything that ever went before. Here the problem is complicated by the fact that the person who once said, 'Never could I love another', and meant it in all sincerity, has now gone and done it.

There are two problems that every couple caught up in a tangle like this have to face. What has happened? What to do about it? We are leaving the whole question of divorce and re-marriage for later consideration, but one can say straight away that the Christian tradition has always been that, in the sense of starting off on a new marriage or breaking off the existing one, *nothing ought to be done about it at all.* There are of course many who will call this an unbearable limitation, but we must just accept the fact that the Christian tradition does say this, and says it for good reasons too. We may perhaps understand some of these reasons if we go more deeply into the question of what has happened. The more old-fashioned religious tradition would have tried to say, either that nothing had happened at all except a foolish illusion, or on the other hand that what had happened was nothing more than 'sin' and so must be treated as such. Neither explanation is at all satisfactory, or is likely to be accepted by the victims of such an affair.

Why can we not admit straight away that it may be a really genuine love-affair? Because we feel that this would be treachery to the one whom we said so firmly was 'the only one'; the one we promised to keep to so exclusively? There is however here a difference between feelings and promises. Feelings we cannot command, we cannot help what they do. But promises we can *make* ourselves keep whatever we happen to feel. 'Treachery' then can only come into the matter of promises; *it cannot enter the domain of feelings at all.*

But why should we *feel* like this all over again? There are two or three questions to be asked here. Have we all actually married the first person we genuinely loved? Many have; but probably a good many more have not. Such people then have quite genuinely loved twice, or even oftener. Ah, but that was before marriage. Quite; but since marriage is a matter of status and legality and will, since it is not made by the emotional feelings, *why should entry into marriage prevent the feelings from falling into love again*? There is no logical reason why it should in theory, and every reason in practice to suppose that it certainly does not. Being married then *of itself* is not a complete barrier to ever falling in love again.

But why should one? Ask again whether or not there is in reality only one person in the world with whom anyone can make a successful and happy marriage. We have already answered that (p. 54), and accepted the suggestion that there are probably half a dozen people with whom, *if one had had to*, one could have made *a* successful marriage. Suppose that one comes across one of these? Are we to suppose that there would be no mutual attraction, nor half-conscious recognition that here was another possible 'complement', at least? And, that recognition being there, it only needs a spark of some trivial kind to set the whole flame of 'love' alight in the emotions. And the very word 'complement' suggests another reason. Since husbands and wives are best in being not exactly alike, in having some characteristics or interests that are not held in common; a meeting with someone who has the qualities which the present spouse lacks may again spark off an affair very easily. Especially as the marriage is likely to be in the stage when the present spouse's qualities are far too much taken for granted.

Need anyone, caught up in an 'eternal triangle', deny at all that they have met someone who *could have been* a partner, who, under different circumstances, *would have been* a partner; and who has perfectly genuinely roused emotional feelings of exactly the same kind as those of the love affair that leads to marriage?

Some such recognition as this is indeed likely to be the first clue as to what to do, how to resolve the problem. For ask now what would be the consequences of leaving the spouse and taking to the 'new love', either by legal divorce and re-marriage or a mere liaison. This is a ticklish subject because it is all very well to suggest that all second marriages of divorcees are unsuccessful; they are not. Many of them are extraordinarily successful and happy; and moralists have got to face this. There are however certain things that can be said without question. One's spouse is not perfect in character, nor the perfect complement, either. Nor is the 'new love'. The imperfections are not likely to be noticed at this stage . . . did one notice those of the spouse when one was engaged? But they are just as truly there, and they may be even more serious, though hidden at the moment under a cloud of glamour and emotional upset combined. But they will appear soon enough. Any union with the 'new love' and off with the present marriage is bound, in its turn, to present exactly similar problems in a few years' time. There is no earthly reason at all (except advancing age) why yet another 'eternal triangle' should not make its appearance and so wreck the second marriage. There is never any guarantee as to what feelings will do for anyone.

Facing these facts, both the fact of the 'genuineness' of the new love-affair, *and* the 'imperfection' that lurks hidden within it just as truly as it lurked in the old, one can see that the calls of duty and fidelity and responsibility have, even from a cynically practical point of view, claims that are almost overwhelming. To make this affair a reason for breaking up the present marriage would seem to be highly dangerous as

well as selfish; extremely risky as well as in some measure
at least partaking of that treachery from which we absolved
the emotions. Nothing then must be done about it except
either get out of it, or resolve it in some fashion that will
do the least hurt. It is possible for some rare people, aided by
the grace of God, to resolve such a situation into a real and
fulfilling friendship between all three. It can be done and it
has been done; but most of us are not able to rise to such a
height. In considering what is the 'least hurt' it is true, however painful it may sound, that the stability of the 'one-flesh-
union' of two-in-one is of more *permanent importance
than the temporary feelings of any one of the three
single individuals.* Some one is bound to get hurt;
but a broken marriage hurts far more than just one
individual.

So much for the first crisis that, in some form or other, is
very likely to arise in most marriages. The second crisis is very
often bound up with this, often indeed it is one of the causes
of an 'outside affair'; but it can also happen quite frequently
on its own.[1] We called it 'the death of love in the marriage';
and that is what it appears to be. Sometimes it is in fact just
this, and a stage has been reached when, humanly speaking,
there is nothing to be done. But very often it is
only an appearance, and people should understand
something of what is likely to happen and see what
can be done when caught up in this kind of apparent
tragedy.

The trouble arises really from two misunderstandings in
which, owing to the false 'glamour-view' of love so pressed
upon us, we are all caught up almost unconsciously. The
first is that we expect the wrong kind of thing from marriage.
Even though we may realize that thrill and glamour will

[1] For a fuller treatment of the religious implications of both these
crises see the author's *The Pattern of Love.*

fade out in due time, we all still expect that personal pleasure will have a large place. And still more that the 'fulfilling of the self', to which we are drawn, *will be a fulfilling of the self in its present form.* Marriage, we think and hope, will make us more of ourselves as we are. It will not; and we may in the end thank God it doesn't. For while limiting us, it will also change and enlarge us as we merge into the 'twy-nature'. But both limitation *and* enlargement *and* change can be painful things; we don't like them while they are happening. 'Death is the gate of Life' may seem a platitudinous religious phrase. (It certainly is so on the lips of many, and especially when regarded as a decorated text to be hung in Victorian bedrooms.) But it has, we know, a deep religious truth as a fact of the spiritual world. And it is equally true of the material world. Since love and marriage partake mysteriously of both these worlds, they should be expected to follow the pattern of truth in both. For it is perfectly true that this 'twy-nature', this 'mystic third person' we talked of in Chapter IV, can only arise out of the partial 'death' of the individuals concerned. If therefore attention and intention in marriage have been largely focused on themselves, they will tend to imagine that, what is in fact only changing them, is killing them. They will cry out that 'love is dead' when in fact love is really struggling to bring a new and different kind of life to birth.

The other misunderstanding is the confusion between the will and the feelings, the emotions and the determination. It is perfectly true that in faithful allegiance to any cause or person—to a political cause, to an ideal, to an art, to God Himself—the will and determination can go on growing while the feelings fluctuate. In the drudgery of artistic training, in the boredom of committees, in the deadliness and dreariness which most of us find in prayer and church-going, there is always given to us an opportunity and a challenge: the opportunity to grow in real allegiance when we don't feel like it, and *the challenge to go on loving when we get nothing out of it.* We expect marriage to be different. But why should it? In point of fact it is not. If we say glibly that we understand that emotion, and even 'love', are not in themselves enough to make marriage grow into a unity, why should we be surprised when we have to experience this; when we have to go through periods, often long years, of boredom and dullness?

So much for theory; what is the practical answer? It is summed up in the word 'faith'; as Anne Ridler says in *The Golden Bird*.[1]

'By faith not feeling is ecstasy commemorated.'

But faith really means two things; determination and memory, and both have to be called to our aid. Determination to make *something* at least out of what appears to be only ruins. And this, as T. S. Eliot says in *The Cocktail Party*, means that in attempting what we think is only 'the best of a bad job', we shall forget all about that, and find a success of a different kind. Different from what we imagined, but possibly even more real. And memory; memory of what the other was in our first wild dreams. For they were quite genuine, those dreams; they were a recognition of that essential reality that lurks behind the changing face of each one of us. The old couple who on their golden wedding-day spent the time 'just looking at each other' were wiser than they knew. They saw each other as they were; they remembered each other as they had been; and they had the faith and the knowledge to realize that behind each facet was the real person they loved. If it is common enough advice to a wife to make herself as attractive to her husband as she can, it is equally good advice to him to try each day and remember her as she looked when he first fell in love with her. For each is the same, and in so far as

[1] Faber and Faber, 1951. p. 30.

they are not the same, it is they who have helped to change each other. They share the responsibility; but common memory can bring the vision back to both.

All, however, do not succeed in overcoming these crises, and so we must turn to the whole subject of divorce and re-marriage and say something about it. And the first thing to say is that there is, widespread in all classes of society to-day, a most pernicious idea that is more responsible than anything else for broken homes and marriages. It is the idea that, because you can get a divorce for adultery, *therefore you must get one as soon as adultery is discovered.* What one may call the cock-eyedness of the modern world was never more completely demonstrated than when a popular newspaper took the Archbishop of Canterbury to task because he stated publicly that he thought that *one act of adultery ought not to be a ground for divorce.* He was more or less accused of condoning sin, of suggesting that sin did not matter. He said nothing of the kind of course; what he did say was that marriage mattered a good deal more. He was also propounding the good old Christian doctrine that, while adultery is a grave sin against marriage, *it does not break or destroy the marriage.* (We might note that, even in the legal sense, it is not the adultery that breaks the marriage. Adultery only gives grounds upon which, *if* the injured party chooses to act, and *if* the law is satisfied as to the injury, then the law may grant a decree. But it is the law, not the adultery, which 'breaks' the marriage.) If we remember all that was said above about the possibility of unfaithfulness being done in act while there was no intention of departure or lack of love of a kind, we shall see that to break a marriage simply and solely because of one act of adultery—or more than one—is being needlessly and stupidly and wilfully precipitate. There are many, many marriages which to-day are on a happy and even keel, which have been through a crisis just like this. One partner has been unfaithful; and has repented. The real underlying causes of the disharmony which caused the act have been unveiled. Both have seen what was wrong and have made a determination to have a fresh start; and so often they have wonderfully succeeded. A marriage breakdown is always a challenge, something to be faced and if possible overcome. Often it is not overcome, of course. But very often it is; and it could be overcome far more often than in fact it is, if people only saw something of the realities involved.

But suppose it is not; suppose that humanly speaking it cannot be. The Christian tradition about marriage has always recognized two things. First, that marriage is of its nature both permanent and exclusive; that is what it is meant to be in theory and ought to be in practice. Secondly, that there do arise cases in which the only thing to do is to separate. Separation of husband and wife, however it may be done legally, has never been condemned in itself as a sin. It may be the only thing to do. The modern world however goes further. It assumes not only that separation is right, but that another marriage may be entered upon after a divorce: and it makes abundant legal provision for this, and not only legal provision, but social and conventional approval.

We must face the fact that Christians differ very profoundly. The Roman Catholic Church has its own rules about what constitutes a valid Christian marriage *for its own members.* If a person who is already a member of that Church goes through a wedding ceremony in any other place than a Roman Catholic Church, their Church does not regard that as a valid Christian marriage. Whatever we may think about that, we ought to recognize that this Church has a right to lay down the law for its own people, and that they know what they are doing, and what is involved, if they choose to break those rules. The Roman Church of course recognizes that, for Christians who are not of the Roman obedience, a valid Christian marriage is entered into whenever two Christians do what is necessary for marriage, whether in another Church or in a State institution. But, once married, the Roman Catholic Church holds that 'a properly constituted and consummated marriage, no power on earth can dissolve'. That is, it absolutely forbids divorce and re-marriage.[1]

The Eastern Orthodox Church has a rather strange discipline in this matter. It reluctantly allows divorce and re-marriage under certain circumstances. It considers that, 'for the hardness of men's hearts', some relaxation of rigidity is required. *But both the divorce and the re-marriage are performed by the Church itself*; and the marriage has to be of a 'penitential nature'. Whatever we may think of this, it is a very different matter from the Church acquiescing in what the State chooses to do; and very different indeed from re-marrying those whom the State, and not the Church, has said are divorced.

The Church of England in its official formularies takes exactly the same line as the Roman Church. Its wedding service, and the Canons by which it is still bound, make it abundantly clear that it does not sanction any re-marriage of those who have been separated—whether by judicial separation or by Decree Absolute. But it is worth noting how the Resolutions of Convocation have worded their requirements that the wedding service is not used for divorced persons. It says that 're-marriage after divorce during the

[1] It would appear however that the Roman Church does not absolutely forbid divorce as such, and regarded merely as a form of separation. See H. J. Davis, S.J., *Moral and Pastoral Theology*: 'Catholics may not under any circumstances petition for an absolute divorce with the intention of remarriage. Catholics may, however, petition for a divorce in the Civil Courts merely in order to obtain the civil effects of a civil divorce.' That is, what is forbidden is, not the separation, however obtained, but any re-marriage. Vol. IV, p. 238, Sheed & Ward, 1949.

life-time of a former partner always involves a departure from the true principle of marriage as declared by our Lord '.[1]

We all know that there are in the Church of England clergy who disagree with this ruling, and an occasional one will be found who, entirely on his own initiative, will approve of such re-marriage and perform the ceremony in church. But the rules are clear, and are at last beginning to be understood. The Church of England however deals very tenderly with people who have broken its rules and have, after divorce, contracted another marriage at a Registrar's office. That however is a *pastoral* matter: it is a method, wise or unwise, of dealing with individuals; it does not affect the principles in the official formularies. The Church of Scotland until recently was willing to approve of the re-marriage of the 'innocent party' and marry such a one in church. It has recently (General Assembly 1957) come to see that the term 'innocent party' is very question-begging, and has ruled that, *under certain conditions*, the re-marriage of any divorced persons may be allowed in church. In many other Christian bodies the question of the official approval of a second marriage—because that is what a wedding in church actually means—is left to the discretion of the individual minister.

Now in all this welter of differing practices and ideas there are two very important things to understand. The first in that the rigidity of some Churches, while it places a discipline upon their own faithful members, who ought to obey what their Church says, *does not pronounce any condemnation on those people who may act differently*. The Church of England Convocation ruling is very carefully worded. It talks about 'a departure from the true principle of marriage as declared

[1] This Resolution, together with several others, was formally declared an Act of Convocation in the Autumn Session, 1957.

by our Lord'; it does not make any specific condemnation of people who may feel that they are justified in making such a breach. After all there are thousands of people who are just ignorant of what Christ's (alleged) teaching is; there are many others who feel in their own consciences that they are justified in what they do. It makes no condemnation of such people; and it makes no pronouncement at all upon the happiness or sincerity of such unions. All it does is to say that, in obedience to what this Church believes are the principles of Christ's teaching, it cannot give official approval and recognition to such unions by a wedding in church. One may presume that the Church of Rome, apart from its own members, would say much the same; for the 'material sin' of such people would be covered by their 'invincible ignorance'. People often talk as if the refusal for instance of the Church of England to marry someone who has been divorced were a *condemnation of that person.* It is not so at all; necessarily. It is merely a statement that the Church thinks that such a union is a 'breach of the principles of Christ's teaching'. Whether a person may be justified or not in his own conscience in committing such a breach, is quite a different matter. That is between his own conscience and God; and no person, or Church, can pronounce on that.

But the other thing to notice is the seriousness with which all Christians view divorce and re-marriage. As C. S. Lewis says somewhere, while the world looks upon marriage as no more than a legal contract which can be made and broken in the same way as any other contract, Christian thought looks on divorce as cutting a living body in two. It is a desperate remedy for desperate cases. Christians may differ as to whether, after what we may call the amputation, it is allowable to graft on a new limb. Some think it cannot be done; others think it may be; but all agree that divorce is like cutting a limb off a living body. Therefore, whether or not the Church to which anyone belongs thinks that divorce and re-marriage may be allowed as a desperate remedy for a desperate case, all Christians ought to go into marriage with the firm idea that, whatever the rest of the world thinks and does, *divorce and re-marriage are not open to them.* It is a plain fact that many people to-day do enter marriage, if not with a conscious eye on the Divorce Court, at least with the unconscious assumption that 'if it doesn't work out we can always have another try'. It is obvious that to have such an assumption at the back of one's mind may mean that the fullest possible effort may not be made to overcome the many crises that crop up in all marriages. And the fact that neighbours and friends may suggest divorce 'because every one does it now' is not going to make the task any easier. A firm resolution that *this way out is not for them* may well prove to be the final thing that keeps them to the sticking point. And no other attitude towards marriage ought to be entertained by any Christians when they enter upon it.

There is one final point. It is often said that the insistence of the Roman and Anglican Churches on no marriage after divorce condemns many of their faithful members to the frustration of life as a single 'person', should their marriage have irretrievably crashed. That is true; and no one ought to attempt to minimize the hardness of the task that is held out to them as the ideal they must try to keep. But there is another side to this. Christianity is never easy over anything; it is not meant to be. It demands a cross somewhere in life, or it is not real Christianity. What of the cross demanded of the many men and women who have never married at all? Of them is demanded chastity, that is refraining from all sexual relationships. And we all know that this is possible, and victoriously practised by a great many men and women. Such people are a standing witness to the Christian demand for chastity. So too can be the divorced or separated who remain unmarried 'for conscience sake'. Those who have been forced to go through the Divorce Court, but who do not avail themselves of their legal, and still more social and conventional, freedom to make another civil marriage—those who voluntarily embrace 'single life' because they do not consider themselves free to re-marry, offer one of the most powerful witnesses to the indissolubility of Christian marriage that it is possible to imagine. And to do this may be the very call of God to some people.

SEVEN

Finale

BEFORE we finally take leave of the Christian beliefs about marriage and sex there are one or two misunderstandings that still need clearing up; for they account a good deal for the fact that people still tend to look askance at the Church in this matter.

There is first the view which Christianity takes of sexual sin. From the very beginning the Christian religion has always looked on unchastity (whether fornication before marriage or adultery after), as a very serious sin. If we are to grant the truth of the various theses we have developed, that idea not only remains, but is really strengthened. Unchastity is not only a grave abuse, it amounts almost to blasphemy . . . however tenderly God may deal with those who sin through ignorance or weakness.

No Christian would, we may hope, wish to go back on this doctrine. Yet it remains true that far too many Christian teachers of all ages have talked as if this were the worst sin of all; indeed sometimes one would imagine it to be the only sin worthy of the name. How many adolescent boys for instance have been terrified out of their minds by thinking that auto-eroticism, which is almost a 'natural' phenomenon at one stage of life, is the terrible and unforgivable 'sin against the Holy Ghost'? And many sincere, but misguided, preachers have encouraged this delusion.

But before condemning biased teaching out of hand, it would be well to remember two facts which have caused the

116

bias. The first is so obvious that none of the critics seem to have noticed it. Sexual sin comes easily to light in a way that other and worse sins do not. If a girl is pregnant when she should not be, everyone can see it. If adultery leads to the Divorce Court everyone knows the names of the parties. This sin therefore is blazoned before the public eye, and is proved to have occurred, in a way that sins of the spirit such as pride, lack of charity, evil-heartedness, etc. never can be. Now if the Church takes disciplinary action over sin, as all Churches once did, at any rate, it can only take action on what is known and proved. It is this fact of public knowledge, rather than any over-censoriousness, which accounts for the fact that ecclesiastical discipline has been, in the popular mind at any rate, associated almost exclusively with sexual sin.

The other reason behind this biased attitude is to be found in that haunting shadow which has hung over the Church in all ages. We call it 'puritanism' sometimes, but that is only one aspect of it. It should really be called 'manichæanism'; a term which will be clear enough to theological students, and to no one else. Nevertheless it is something very important. When the Christian religion appeared in the world and began to spread, there was already very widespread in the religious consciousness of mankind an idea that anything connected with the material world or the body was essentially evil. It is an Eastern idea; it springs from the '*maya*' or illusion of all things that is taught by Hinduism. Any such idea is of course clean contrary to the Christian belief in the Incarnation. It would seem that the Gospel of St John was specifically written to combat such ideas; hence the insistence in the Prologue that *the Word was made flesh*. The Church fought this idea to the death—officially. But it could not prevent its shadow creeping in all the same. The excessive cult of virginity in the Middle Ages was one result. (Note the word 'excessive'; virginity itself, as we shall see, has an

honourable place in Christianity). This Puritanism or Janse-
nism which despises and loathes the body has never quite
been expelled from popular Christianity. No two religious
systems could seem to be more opposed to each other than
the dour Calvinism of ancient Scotland and the popular
Catholicism of modern Ireland. Yet their attitude to sex is
almost exactly the same; it consists of a sort of fascinated
horror.

What then is the truth? All departures from that perfection
demanded by God, all departure from compliance with His
laws, is sin. But there are degrees of sin (see I John 5.17).
Sins of the spirit can be, and usually are, far more soul-
destroying and corrupting than sins of the body. To indulge
the sensations of the flesh may well be far less separating
from God than to indulge such passions of the spirit as pride
or hate or wicked independence. There is really only one way
in which sins of the flesh are to be specially noted. While not
being the worst of sins they are typical of the very nature of
sin. For in sexual sin it is as if a person said to God: 'You
gave me these powers for your purposes. I am going to use
them entirely for my own pleasure'. Sex may not be the worst
way of disobeying God; weakness or ignorance may remove a
large proportion of the guilt; but to say and mean this is of
the very essence of all sin.

To the modern world which has left the Christian demands
so very far behind, we need to say very firmly that unchastity
is sin. But it is also necessary to tell many Christians that it is
not the worst of sins, and to warn them that the chaste may
often be in far worse spiritual danger than the unchaste.

But this brings up a second thing over which there is perhaps even more misunderstanding. That is the proper
Christian attitude towards pleasure. It may well be that the
Puritan attitude towards sex stems from its ingrained belief
in the wickedness of pleasure; that sex is viewed as wrong

primarily because its exercise inevitably causes pleasure. For to the Puritan mind pleasure is always suspect; with the result that to the popular mind in this country Christianity is still thought of primarily as something that stops you doing everything that you want to do. How many chaste and virtuous people still have a sort of a guilty conscience when they discover that the proper use of sex in marriage is pleasurable? They feel that somehow this ought not to be so, or that if they were 'really devout' they would be above such feelings.

This is a truly dreadful attitude, but to resolve it is not as easy as it appears. After all Christianity does demand self-sacrifice, it calls for a cross in life and for renunciation. It is only too true that it very frequently happens that the thing which we desperately want to do is just the very thing which we ought *not* to do; that the will of God is the thing we would prefer not to do or happen. It is no good pretending that this is not so. In this over-materialistic world this truth needs preaching—and indeed practising—pretty strongly. But we need to be very wary of seeming to give the impression that this is always so. It is not; and there are times when God calls us to serve Him by doing the very thing which we most desire to do.

What we really need of course is a whole theology of pleasure into which we can fit the pleasures of sex. But it may well be that a study of the subject of sexual pleasure would shed light on the whole problem. A young couple who are deeply in love desire more than anything else to make love to each other in the full and proper sense. Such a desire is both natural and right in itself. We know too that unless they are ultimately going to be able to do this their love will be both frustrated and lessened. But until they are actually married Christianity says very firmly that they ought not to do what they so much want to do.

But what happens when they are married? The situation has then completely changed. They will still want to make love, even more so, probably. But, now that they are actually married, this thing which they desire so much (whose potential pleasure has so attracted them) is the very thing which God Himself intends that they shall do. It is the very thing out of which He is going to bring to birth the new ' twy-nature '; the thing by which He is going to make them into one. To make love now is to fulfil God's twin purposes of creation and fulfilment. *Not to do it now would be to go against the purposes of God.*

If then it is right and proper for the lovers to perform this act is there any reason why they should not enjoy it to the full? If sexual intercourse is now part of the glory of the vocation of serving God, surely any attempt to cut out the joy is really a failure in response. More: it is a failure in worship; for it is not for nothing that the *Book of Common Prayer* of the Church of England tells the bridegroom that he is to say to his bride: ' With my body I thee worship.' Praying, as C. S. Lewis says, can include playing, and indeed ought to do so. Is it perhaps because the modern world has so forgotten the praying part that it gets so little satisfaction out of the playing part?

For far too long have we restricted that word ' worship ' to what is done in church . . . and there is too often done in a dull and merely conventional way.

' To eat when we are hungry, to drink when we thirst, to dance, to sing, to cleave the water with a strong arm is to praise and glorify God. To run, to ride, to swim, to sleep when the day's work is over . . . all, all is worship . . . in all God is praised and glorified '.[1]

[1] Address on ' The Principles of Christian Worship ' by the Rev Charles Walsham Hutchinson. *Anglo-Catholic Congress Papers*, 1927.

Was it not the late Fr Neville Figgis of Mirfield who said once that the saddest moments in the atheist's life were not when he had no one to appeal to in sorrow, but when he had no one to thank for joy? To those who use their bodies for the purposes and the glory of God there can be given a joy, and a pleasure even, that the sensualist must forever miss.

But all men and women do not get married; what has Christianity to say about sex that can be applied to all? Simply this; that since our sexual powers are a gift from God that should be returned to Him in response and worship, what we do with them ought always to be in response to a vocation or call of some kind. And there are in fact for a Christian only three possible vocations over sex. One is marriage, and we may call this the ' using ' of sex since it is the functioning of sexual powers for their proper purposes under the proper conditions.

But there is another call or vocation which comes to some, which we might call, not the using, but the ' renunciation ' of sex. In church language it is called *celibacy*. That is the deliberate giving up of the use of sex in response to some other and different call. This might be the call to such an utter dedication of life to the service of God as demands also the giving up of such other human rights as property and freedom of choice. Such is the call to the life of those who are dedicated by the monastic vows of poverty, chastity and obedience. But it might very well be a call to some ' secular ' profession or kind of work which is incompatible with marriage in general, or which precludes marriage for the person in question. Obviously the people to whom such calls will come are, and always will be, a minority; this is a call to a special kind of work, whether secular or religious, that involves a more than ordinary commitment. But the possibility of such special calls coming to some people ought only to emphasize the fact that the 'normal vocation' of marriage involves an equally total commitment of life and person.

Some then are called to use sex, and some to renounce it; but what of the rest? What of those who are still waiting to be called to one or other of these? Surely the third vocation might be described as that of 'guarding sex.' This works in two ways. Young men and women to whom the call to marriage has not yet come, but who do not feel that they are called to renounce sex for ever, are yet called upon to renounce it temporarily for the sake of the marriage that may come in the future. 'Guarding' rather than renunciation is the word for them, for this is precisely what they are doing, guarding their powers for a probable future fulfilment.

But there will always be those whom marriage has apparently just passed by. The bachelors and the spinsters who have never received any special call to renunciation, but to whom the fulfilment of marriage has just never come. Any hope of it has apparently long gone by. They too are called to keep and guard their sexuality by not using it. Not because someone else may one day appear to claim it, but as a witness to the world of what Christian chastity is, what it means and demands. The superficial world is always trying to say that chastity is 'impossible'. It may grant the possibility to un-usual people like religious celibates perhaps, but to normal people? The witness of the bachelors and spinsters who are perfectly normal, who have no call to extraordinary vocations, is of immense value in these days. It may be of incalculable value to many young men and women who are waiting for marriage, and thus it can play an enormous part of guarding the sanctity of marriage for others. This is exactly the point of the Christian doctrine of vicarious sacrifice. To be forced to remain unmarried is a sacrifice, and let no one attempt to minimize this, but it is a sacrifice which may well have an enormous effect on the lives of others. *It need never be a merely barren sacrifice.* There was a lecturer once who shattered an audience consisting largely of spinster school-mistresses by telling them that the single life was a 'martyrdom'. But he picked up the brick he seemed to have dropped by telling them that, as a married man, he could say that marriage was also a martyrdom. That shocked the rest of the audience; but it is perfectly true. Both single life and married life are a 'martyrdom' in the proper sense of that word, which is that of a 'witness'. Both are a witness to Christianity; and each has its own peculiar limitations and sacrifices, and each its own peculiar joys and freedoms. What really matters is the *acceptance* of either. As regards single life that comes unsought and unwished this acceptance is what the psychologists call sublimation. And as such it prevents frustration. It leads in the end to fulfilment, but fulfilment of a different kind.

Neither the single life nor the married life leads automatically to fulfilment; if there are soured bachelors and spinsters around us, there are also many wrecked marriages. Neither leads just by itself to God. But each way can, if only God is put first. The Church in the past has seemed to stress the fact that the detachment of single life can be a very direct road to God. So of course it can, as St Paul was never tired of saying. But it is high time that we stressed the other fact, that marriage *and its very involvement in the life of another*, can also lead direct to God. 'Losing oneself in another' which is of the very essence of happy and successful marriage, may indeed be the way by which the majority of people are meant to learn . . . and to work out in daily life . . . the truth that salvation means in the end losing oneself in The Other Who is God.

For to the Christian *limitation always means in the end*

enlargement. Here we can perhaps approach a matter which has already been referred to in two footnotes; the matter of second marriage after the death of a previous partner. There is no doubt that the early Church looked very askance at such practices. (It is reported that the Orthodox Church, which demands that secular priests be married, also refuses to ordain a man who has married again after being widowed.) It seems that Christianity, for all its insistence upon one man to one woman being the divine pattern, with its idea that the image of God can only be found in the unique couple exclusively bound to each other, has also said that this is not an absolute and utterly complete exclusiveness. Death, which is an 'Act of God', does open a wider door. The clue to understanding this probably lies in those strange words of Jesus: 'In the resurrection they neither marry nor are given in marriage' (Matt. 22.30). These words have undoubtedly troubled many. They have been taken to mean either that marriage is some sort of concession to carnal life with no place in what is really spiritual, or, even more disastrously, that we shall not in heaven have any special relation to our spouses . . . even perhaps that we shall not recognize them or need them.

All this is to look at these words from the point of view of limitation. But if limitation means enlargement, there is a totally different meaning that can be got from them. We once called marriage and love a 'special case' of the general rule of divine charity to all men (p. 56). Presumably in the full divine interchange of love in heaven there will be no special case. But this is simply because all special cases will have been swallowed up in the unimaginable fullness of love that flows between God and all the Redeemed, and between all of them together. What on earth was limited, and rightly limited, to one person, may there, with no diminution whatever of the intimate love for one, be shared with many . . . ultimately

with all because it is also shared with God. The allowability
of second marriage on earth after God himself has removed
the previous limitation, does mean that for people in those
circumstances, there can be already an experience of a
'one-flesh union' with more than one person. The circumstances are peculiar, unique, and not of their making. But
the experience of those who are in such a position is surely
that the second union and love do not in any way diminish
the reality of the first. Is this a parable as it were, a
faint foreshadowing, of what we are all meant to come to
eventually?

Presumably there will not be sex in heaven. But this is not
because sex is evil, merely that it is earthly. While we are
human beings on this earth this intimate union, which is
based on and arises out of the sexual division and union
of humanity, must be limited. But through the limited, and
through our acceptance of the limitations, we are to be
enlarged and rise to 'higher things'. 'Higher' yes; but, for
the vast majority, for those called to marriage, all that is
higher rises out of their sexual union.

This may all sound terribly theoretical and even theological;
but it is in the end intensely practical. For the whole thing
follows a pattern; a pattern of pointers and limitations, of
the lesser all the time included in the greater, of limitation
leading always to enlargement. The pattern can be followed
all the way through from the first stirring of sexual desire,
through sex attraction and the storms of calf-love, on to
romantic love and the call to marriage, and then on through
the formation of the family-community, substitution and
living in another. Desire turns to passion, passion to tenderness, tenderness to charity, yet not one of them ever loses its
reality.

It is a straight road, but a narrow one; there are side turn-
ings innumerable, *ersatz* satisfactions that turn sour, snacks

that masquerade as feasts, but to those who will follow the pattern of endless limitation and enlargement it leads to the goal. Man has taken sex and used it to send himself on a road that seems too often to lead towards hell; but God gave us sex as one of the roads that might lead us to heaven itself.

Index